THE FLAME
OF ADVENTURE

Born in Leicestershire in 1963, Simon Yates first came to prominence as a mountaineer in 1985, after the first ascent of the West Face of Siula Grande and the ensuing epic descent with Joe Simpson – described in Simpson's book *Touching the Void*. Since then he has travelled extensively in India, Pakistan, Nepal, Kazakhstan, South America and Australia, and has climbed new routes in the Himalayas and the Andes, sometimes acting as a mountain guide. His first book, *Against the Wall*, was runner up in the Boardman Tasker Award for mountaineering literature. Simon now lives in Cumbria and makes a living from running commercial expeditions (www.mountaindream.co.uk) and lecturing.

ALSO BY SIMON YATES

Against the Wall

Simon Yates

THE FLAME
OF ADVENTURE

V

VINTAGE

Published by Vintage 2002

6 8 10 9 7 5

First published in Great Britain in 2001 by
Jonathan Cape

Vintage
Random House, 20 Vauxhall Bridge Road,
London SW1V 2SA

Random House Australia (Pty) Limited
20 Alfred Street, Milsons Point, Sydney,
New South Wales 2061, Australia

Random House New Zealand Limited
18 Poland Road, Glenfield, Auckland 10,
New Zealand

Random House (Pty) Limited
Endulini, 5A Jubilee Road, Parktown 2193,
South Africa

The Random House Group Limited Reg. No. 954009
www.randomhouse.co.uk

A CIP catalogue record for this book
is available from the British Library

ISBN 0 099 28386 7

Papers used by Random House are natural, recyclable products made from wood grown in sustainable forests. The manufacturing processes conform to the environmental regulations of the country of origin

Printed and bound in Great Britain by
Bookmarque Ltd, Croydon, Surrey

In memory of Mark and Tony

Contents

Illustrations

Alan Wilkie in Snell's Field, Chamonix, France. (Photo: Simon Yates)

Joe Simpson on the North Face of the Aiguille Blanc de Peuterey, Italy. (Photo: Yates)

Looking down on John Silvester climbing the Second Icefield on the North Face of the Eiger, Switzerland. (Photo: Yates)

John Silvester on the summit ridge of the Eiger, (Photo: Yates)

Leyla Peak, northern Pakistan. We climbed up to a gully to breach the rock band in the bottom right of the picture, before moving back left to join the snow ridge. (Photo: Steve Razzetti)

Looking up at Tom Curtis and Andy Cave tackling the gully on Leyla Peak. (Photo: Yates)

On the Summit of Leyla Peak – Simon, Tom Curtis, Andy Cave and Sean Smith. (Photo: Yates)

Mark Miller in front of the damaged Leicester University jeep, Pakistan. (Photo: Mike Searle)

The Biale Expedition at base camp. Standing: Captain Naveed, our liaison officer, Sean Smith, Nick Groves, Simon and Mary Rose Fowlie. Sitting: Mike Searle, Mark Miller and Haqeem, our cook. (Photo: Sean Smith)

The South Face of Baile. We climbed diagonally leftwards

from the basin to the snowy col and then followed the ridge above. (Photo: Searle)

Nick Groves climbing high on Lobsang II. Mustagh Tower and K2 are behind. (Photo: Smith)

Sean Smith reaching the col on Biale. Behind are K2, Mustagh Tower, Broad Peak, Gasherbrum IV and Gasherbrum I. (Photo: Yates)

Looking west from the col at the Great Trango Tower and Nameless Tower, with Uli Biaho behind. (Photo: Yates)

Typical country in the foothills of eastern Nepal. (Photo: Yates)

Anne Murray below the south face of Kanchenjunga after our epic trek through the jungle. (Photo: Yates)

Ruined temple in Hampi, India. (Photo: Yates)

Anne's motorbike in a small northern Thai Village. (Photo: Yates)

Joe Simpson re-enacting our Peruvian drama for American TV in the Buguboos, Canadian Rockies. (Photo: Yates)

Kevin tends to his truck crossing the Nullabor Plain, Australia. (Photo: Yates)

Simon rock climbing at Mount Arapiles, Victoria, Australia. (Photo: Yates)

Simon and Sean Smith admiring the fields of Nagar on the walk in to the Hispar, northern Pakistan. (Photo: Searle)

Guiding in Scotland. The aftermath of the minibus crash. (Photo: Yates)

Access work on the Broadgate Development, London. (Photo: Pat McVey)

Our Christmas tree at Nanga Parbat base camp, northern Pakistan. The tangerines were frozen solid. (Photo: Yates)

Arbat Street, Moscow. (Photo: Yates)

Khan Tengri above the International Camp, Soviet Kazakhstan. (Photo: Yates)

Members of the Russian National Mountaineering Squad sunbathing at base camp after a storm. (Photo: Yates)

Near the summit of Khan Tengri. (Photo: Yates)

Simon on the summit of Khan Tengri. (Photo: Smith)

In these days of upheaval and violent change, when the basic values of today are the vain and shattered dreams of tomorrow, there is much to be said for a philosophy which aims at living a full life while the opportunity offers. There are few treasures of more lasting worth than the experience of a way of life that is in itself wholly satisfying. Such, after all, are the only possessions of which no fate, no cosmic catastrophe can deprive us; nothing can alter the fact if for one moment in eternity we have really lived.

Eric Shipton, *Upon That Mountain*

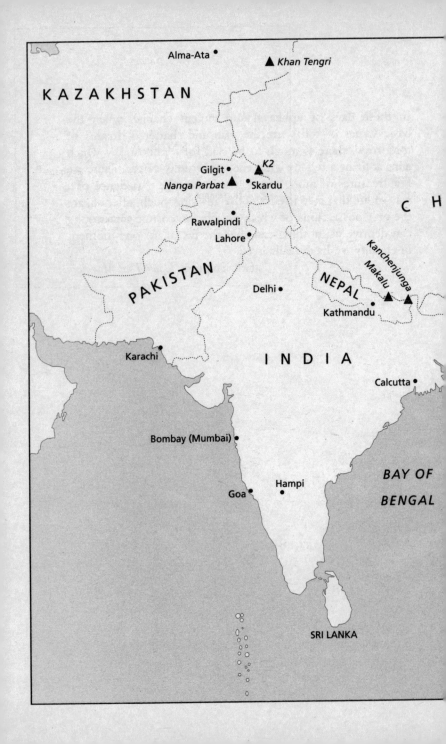

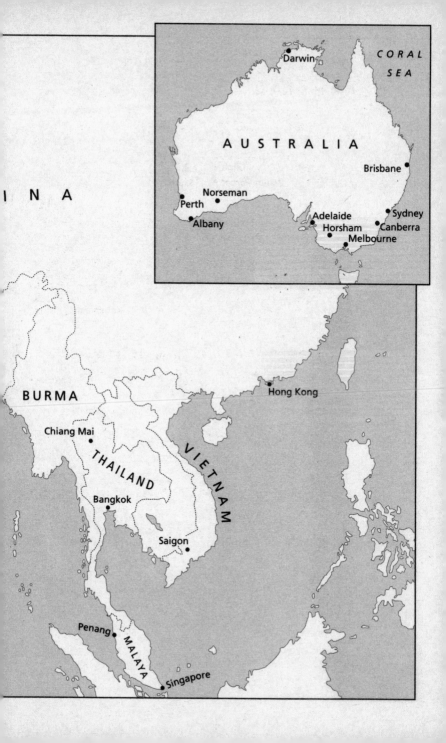

Introduction

Different Rules

I slumped forward into the slope and let my body weight drop on to the ski-poles I held in each hand. The poles sank deeply into the soft, wet snow reducing me to an uncomfortable stoop. Normally I would have plunged them in again and readjusted myself into a more upright position, but I was too tired to care. I simply stood bowed, head down, listening to my gasping breath. My heart was pounding and with each beat, painful pulses of blood ran through bulging veins on either side of my forehead. Beads of sweat ran down my face and soaked into the cotton scarf tied around my head to protect me from the glaring sun. In the rarefied air it was difficult to take adequate breaths. It felt as if my lungs were going to collapse. My heart hurt from its exertions and despite regular application of high-factor sun cream the fierce sunlight was burning my skin. Even the insides of my nostrils were tingling. Rolling my tongue around the inside of my mouth I felt sticky lumps of dried saliva, reminding me that the water bottle I had painstakingly filled with melted snow the previous night had been empty for some time. I was desperately thirsty.

When we had left our tents a couple of hours before dawn to start climbing, the temperature had been well below freezing with a bitter wind blowing. It had been necessary to put on a down jacket to stay warm. At the coldest time around sunrise, I had to stop regularly to blow into my chilled hands and warm them up.

Eventually, the sun crept above the surrounding peaks bringing welcome warmth. However, as it rose higher, temperatures soared. It seemed as if the slopes in the valley I was climbing were acting as a huge magnifying glass with me at its focus. The snow rapidly softened and although others were in front breaking trail, I often sank through their steps to up above my knees. I started to shed clothing, but quickly reached a point where all I was wearing was a thermal top and a pair of fleece trousers. I would have happily removed the lot, but I knew from bitter experience what the sunlight would do to pale exposed skin. At times in the past I had been so badly sunburned that my skin blistered and developed into horrible weeping sores.

It seemed ironic that here, high on a large snowy mountain, the biggest problem I faced was the heat. Most people would imagine high mountains to be cold and inhospitable places. However, many of the world's tallest peaks lie in warm climatic zones and they can be exceptionally hot. I have been at both my coldest and hottest whilst climbing mountains. It is the heat that I find harder to deal with. At least when it gets cold you can put on more clothing. I had reached the limit of what I could take off and carrying the spare clothes was simply making me overheat more. But more than anything it was the sheer intensity of the sunlight that I found most tiring. Like strong wind, its effect is psychological. It gets inside your mind, somehow numbing the senses. After a time you simply long to escape from the constant glare and to step into the comfort of the shade.

Slowly my gasps for breath subsided and I reached a point where I could breathe normally. This was my cue to start moving again. I pulled out the ski-poles, plunged them into the slope above and began, silently cursing whoever had gone first for having long legs. I had to take big ungainly strides to follow the trail in the snow.

The movement generated a rhythm of its own. For most of the time I simply kept my head down and counted steps. Presently I was managing forty between rests, but after a particularly long rest, or with concerted effort I could push it up to fifty. Occasionally I played with the number of steps, or hummed tunes to the time of my walking. But I knew that if I did not count I would naturally stop earlier and my progress would be slower.

At my next rest I stared down, tracing the trail of steps along the small valley I had been following. A lone figure – my friend Sean Smith – was moving barely perceptibly along a flat section some way below. I estimated he was perhaps half an hour behind me. He looked tiny and vulnerable with the huge, icy North Face of Pik Pobeda soaring above him. Our hosts and guides to the area – a group of Russian climbers – were somewhere above. Being fitter and better acclimatised they had left us behind. We had caught only glimpses of them since leaving camp earlier in the day. Not that I was worried. I knew what line our chosen route took up the mountain and we would meet up with them again in the evening at the next camp, if not earlier.

Down below Sean, the ground dropped away steeply on to the glacier where we had started our climb. From this height the striations in the ice and ridges of moraines on top of it looked like vessels inside a living organism. Further down, the glacier joined another much larger one. I could just make out tiny specks of colour at the junction, which were the tents of our base camp.

At the top of the larger glacier stood the pyramidal peak of Khan Tengri. Sean and I had climbed to the summit just a few days before. It was a photograph of the peak that had brought us to the range of mountains in the first place. Before then I had not heard of the Tien Shan range, let alone known their location, which spanned Kazakhstan, Kirghizia and Western China in Central Asia.

Khan Tengri was stunningly beautiful. Its symmetry was near perfect – two triangular-shaped faces split by an arrow-straight ridge. The peak was also high and at 6,995 metres the second largest in the Tien Shan range. Only Pik Pobeda, the mountain we were now attempting, was higher. At sunset one of the faces glowed a peachy orange while the other was in shade. Even now in the bright light of the day the peak looked too perfect to be natural. The mountain's beauty hypnotised me. I saw myself climbing that perfect ridge and wondered how it would compare to the route we had climbed.

I shook my head, a little disgusted with myself for allowing so much time to pass. It was only mid-morning and there was at least another thousand metres of climbing to reach the camp at around 6,500 metres. The heat, exertion and lack of oxygen were already getting to me. It was going to be a long tiring day.

Just as I started moving again the silence was broken by a bang. The sudden sound was immediately followed by a much more sinister rumbling. I stopped in my tracks and looked around, scanning the steep face above. I knew exactly what I was looking for and it only took a few seconds to find the source of the sound. About half way up the face was an avalanche. It had broken off some ice-cliffs a little higher and was speeding down the face.

Despite being threatening, the boiling mass of powder snow was compelling to look at and it grew in width and depth as it fell. Then I remembered Sean. The avalanche was heading towards where I had last seen him. I looked back down the valley but he must have been hidden behind one of the many small crests. I could not see him. Then I looked up again. The avalanche was still growing and nearly at the bottom of the face. When it hit the flat it bubbled up further, but quickly dissipated. It was carrying much less snow than I had first thought. Sean was safe. At times it was easy to forget the danger when surrounded by so much beauty.

I followed the line of steps, steadily gaining height, pulling up out of the small valley on to a blunt, rounded ridge.

The lower section was mostly snow, but I could see above was steeper with more rocky sections. The views became increasingly spectacular, but I grew more exhausted and less able to appreciate them. By now I was getting concerned. Sean was below, but I had seen no further sign of the Russians. There was no obvious camp on the ridge above. Rationally, I knew I could not have gone off route but doubt was beginning to creep into my mind. I started looking around, hoping to find a camp hidden by boulders or tucked away in some unlikely spot. It simply had to be near.

As I began to get seriously worried, I suddenly spotted a small red flag sticking out of the snow just below the more broken rocky ground.

As I approached the flag I realised it marked the entrance to a snow hole. The hole was the width of a person and about waist height. I took off my rucksack and, crouching down, shuffled inside. The tunnel opened out into an enormous chamber which was above head height. Here it was possible to move around quite freely. About twenty Russians were spread out inside, but there was room for many more. At the back of the chamber, raised platforms acted as beds and at the front, people were cooking with stoves in compartments that had been cut into the wall.

Some of the Russians nodded to acknowledge me, but I simply stood silently in the corner of the chamber watching what was going on. This sort of set-up in the mountains was beyond my experience. The snow holes I had made myself had been tiny affairs that had accommodated a maximum of four people. They were so time-consuming to dig that I had never bothered to made them high enough to stand in. Days of work had gone into this room.

Someone handed me a cup of tea and I sat down. Two men were working at the far end of the cave with shovels, enlarging the hole still further, others were laying out sleeping mats and some were sorting through equipment. All the activity made me feel guilty.

'Wow,' said Sean as he burst in through the entrance a little later. 'Some snow hole.'

'I know,' I replied. 'People live in houses smaller than this.'

'Colder as well,' he pointed out. With all the people inside the place was so warm that water was dripping from the melting ceiling.

Our hosts left shortly after we arrived. It seemed as though we were going to spend the entire expedition trying to keep up with them. I wondered if they found us weak or lazy. After a second cup of tea Sean pointed to the door.

'We'd better get going,' he said. 'It's beginning to cloud up and you know how bad the weather can be here.'

'Sure.' I remembered a storm earlier in our trip that had confined us to our tent for days, during which time a metre of snow had fallen.

We stepped outside into a biting wind. The sun was still shining, but dark threatening clouds were now starting to fill the sky from the west. I dropped back into my routine of forty steps, deep breathing and then a short rest. The ground steepened and sections of rope fixed into place hung down short rock buttresses.

I had not expected the climbing to be so steep. It was possible to climb the rock without the aid of the ropes, but I unashamedly pulled on them to go faster. However, I soon passed a place where the rope had been severed and tied together again. Sections of the rope were so badly abraded that only a few strands of core the thickness of string remained. I was amazed that the Soviet climbers who put the rope in place had not kept it to a higher standard. It was some of the worst rope I had ever seen. I soon stopped using it, reasoning it was safer to climb up myself rather than pull on a rope that was likely to break and cause a fall.

The climbing became absorbing, not just a matter of following footsteps in the snow. The route turned corners, weaved round towers of rock and through bands of little overlaps, and all the time the sky darkened and the wind increased. A look at my watch told me it was getting late. In a little over an hour's time it would be getting dark. I was very tired. We needed to reach the camp and to set up our tent and a rumble of thunder only added to the sense of urgency.

As the hailstones started thudding on to my clothing and rucksack, I saw the camp. Not far above at the side of a large boulder was the distinctive red tunnel tent. The sky darkened further, then a flash of lightning momentarily lit the sky, followed almost immediately by a deafening crack of thunder. I tried to quicken my pace, but my body would not respond. The hailstones were now falling so heavily that I could barely see where I was going and the wind knocked me first one way then another. It was a huge relief when I finally reached my destination.

I crouched down outside and tried to find a way in. Unlike the tents I was familiar with, it had no zip. In fact the entrances were like windsocks stitched on to the sides of the tent and pulled tight by drawcords. The ends of the cords were inside. Someone must have heard me, as a windsock opened and a head appeared outside.

'Come in,' said Sergei his face grimacing in the wind and hail, 'quick.'

Without hesitation I dived inside. A welcome ring of smiling faces greeted me. The roar of the storm was instantly replaced by another coming from gas stoves. I removed my rucksack, added it to a pile by the entrance and made myself comfortable.

It was nice to be out of the storm, but more than anything it was good to stop. It had been a very long day. I calculated we had climbed about 1,700 metres. It was by far the biggest height gain I had ever made at altitude in a single day and I was suffering as a result. My limbs and head ached and for the first time I noticed the sunburn on my face. The Russians by contrast all looked relaxed, showing little of the strain that is usually etched on people's faces while climbing at those heights. While two worked the stoves, others were reading. Irena, the only woman in their team, was busy giving a head massage.

'Where will you all sleep?' I asked Sergei, noticing how little spare space there was in the tent, even with everyone sitting up.

'Here,' he waved his arm in an arc.

To me it seemed bizarre to spend a night crammed into a tent with so many others after such a hard day's climbing and the prospect of several more days to come. I could not see how they were going to sleep and imagined they would get dangerously tired as the climb went on.

'And you?' asked Sergei.

'Our small tent.'

Sergei nodded knowingly. He had questioned our use of the two-man tent on the previous mountain. We were finding each other's methods of climbing puzzling.

Later, after Sean had arrived, Irena gave us both head massages. As she gently rubbed around my eyes and temples I felt the pressure that had built up across my forehead during the day gradually subsiding. Then we watched preparations for dinner. To our amazement fresh vegetables were produced from rucksacks. Carrots and potatoes were added to a casserole, while a salad of tomatoes and cucumber was made. The only potatoes I had ever taken up a mountain were dried ones and I had never even considered taking salad.

We pitched our tent above the Russian camp, as the sun set bloodily behind a bank of boiling cloud which flickered with lightning in the gathering darkness.

'Did you see what they were eating?' I asked as we made a meal of instant noodles.

'Yeah. They must be mad carrying that lot.'

It was not a good night. We were both troubled by headaches and in the incessant wind found it difficult to sleep. It was a relief when the alarm woke us early the next morning. The weather had cleared in the night, but the wind was still blowing. It was very cold. We went through the ritual of melting snow for drinks in silence. Neither of us could face eating. Finally, we put on our clothes and boots and left the tent.

The Russians were already out in the open. I waved at them and wondered if their night had been any better than ours. We hurriedly collapsed the tent, packed it away and started climbing. I soon began to move away from Sean, who was not going well. After an easy section following the crest of the low-angled ridge, a trail of steps led off almost horizontally to the left and disappeared around a steep buttress. As I traversed across towards it I looked back down and saw that a group of the Russians had overtaken Sean. This was no surprise and I knew it would not be long before they did the same to me.

On the other side of the buttress a rope ran up a steep basin of snow to the right side of a pillar of rock. The rope followed the pillar for some way before disappearing over a bulging icy wall. Like those lower down, the ropes were not in the best of condition. In the snow basin I was able to climb without really pulling on them, but once I reached the rock it was impossible. Reluctantly, I unclipped the Russian jumar from my harness and looked at it. It was poorly finished and did not inspire confidence. I cursed myself for forgetting my own, while I attached the device to the rope.

The jumar, connected to my harness by a nylon sling, would slide up the rope but not back down. By pulling on the rope with one hand and then sliding the jumar upwards with the other I could gain height and then rest my weight on the rope between moves.

I began the rhythmical movement, making several quick steps upwards before slumping on to the rope for a rest. The Russians accompanying us appeared from the other side of the buttress and, without pausing, started to climb the ropes below. I thought little about them and carried on. It was only when climbing the bulging icy wall towards the top of the difficulties that I noticed them again. As I sat resting in my harness, the rope suddenly lurched downwards. For a few moments my heart pounded and I looked down to see one of the Russians attached to the same rope I was already climbing. I was horrified. The rope was in poor condition and I felt uncomfortable hanging on it myself, let alone sharing it with another climber. In addition I had always followed the protocol that only one person climbed a section of fixed rope at any given time. Now there were two of us.

'Stop! Get off the rope,' I yelled at the man below, waving frantically. He looked up, paused momentarily and continued.

'No. Stop,' I tried again. To me my safety concerns seemed obvious. With two on the same dubious rope it was much more likely to break or its anchor fail.

By now it was clear that I was not going to get the Russian off my section of rope, so I set out to climb faster. I knew that above there would be a belay that I could secure myself to and let him past. Then suddenly there was another jerk on the rope, which stretched noticeably. Another climber had joined us.

'Noooo,' I screamed, waving again at the two below. They looked at me as though I had somehow lost my mind. To me there was now extreme danger for all of us, but to them it seemed like there was none. I kept shouting and waving, but they ignored me and simply carried on up the rope. When the lead Russian climber reached a point just a few metres below me, he waved me on dismissively. As it was difficult to pass until we reached a belay, there was little I could do but obey his command.

I turned my attention back to the wall of ice above and completed a series of rapid heaves on the rope, simultaneously skipping up with my crampons. The higher I climbed, the more iced-up the rope became, and it became increasingly difficult to make progress with the large mitts I was wearing. With each movement both from myself and those below, I felt tension ripple along the thin cord, which flattened and stretched before my eyes.

Quickly regaining my breath I moved up again, over the steepest section of ice. Not far above was a belay. I knew

I was almost out of danger, so I pushed myself until my lungs started to scream. Eventually I could go no further and slumped on to the rope for a rest, but it did not hold me. Something was wrong. I started falling. I flipped upside down and began to feel a sensation of speed as my vision blurred. Then suddenly I stopped.

The fall had been short – about five metres – and I was now back at the bottom of the icy wall. A Russian was just below me. He looked puzzled, but quickly started climbing again. There was a fiery pain in my right ankle. I tried to put my weight on to it, but it hurt too much. I was going to have to go down, although as the Russians struggled to get past me I could not figure out how.

I cursed the Russians for hanging on the rope and myself for forgetting my own jumar. It had been a combination of these two factors that had caused my fall. I had never known jumars to slip before, even on iced-up ropes. However, I had been forced to borrow one having left my own in the base camp. The Russian jumar was made differently from western ones and did not have teeth on the cam that gripped the rope. It had been this, and the others below pulling the icy rope taut, which had caused the device to slip. Fortunately, after the short drop the cam had gripped the rope again and held my fall. If I had fallen further I would have run into one or more of the climbers below and knocked them off. The resulting falls would have put further strain on the rope and belay, making them more likely to fail. We had all been very lucky.

The Russians continued to stream past me. I managed somehow to slide down the rope to a belay below and waited for them to go past. Sean came around the steep buttress and into my sight.

'I've had an accident,' I shouted down. 'Wait there for a while. I'm coming back.'

Once the last Russian had passed me I started abseiling down the rope. As the angle eased I had to put more weight on my legs and the pain in my ankle increased. I hopped and dragged myself back along the rope towards Sean.

'What happened?' he asked as I got close to him.

'My jumar slipped and I took a short fall. I think I might have broken my ankle.'

'What a bummer. It's not going to be easy getting down from here.'

'I know,' I replied, well aware of the difficulty I had found simply reaching him. To escape I now faced over two thousand metres of descent to the glacier and several kilometres of walking back to the base camp.

With Sean's help I was able to stagger back to the top camp, but it was agonising and time-consuming. Eventually we reached the Russian tent and dived inside.

'What has happened?' asked Sergei, surprised by our return.

'I have fallen, I think my ankle may be broken.' I felt angry and wanted to complain to him about the irresponsibility of the others climbing up the rope below me, but there was no point. They would not understand. They had their way of doing things and we had ours. It was becoming clearer as we spent more time here in the Soviet Union that our ways of doing things were quite different.

'We will help,' Sergei said without hesitation.

I lay back and relaxed for a while. My foot was throbbing with pain. There was a flurry of conversation between the Russians, before Sergei began to speak into a walkie-talkie. I sat up, wrestled my boot off and pulled down my socks to expose the ankle. The sight brought a few sympathetic gasps from the others in the tent. It was hideously swollen. There was further activity with the radio.

'Another team are coming down. They will be here in one hour. They will help you down,' Sergei explained. 'Now we go up.' They began packing their rucksacks and preparing to leave.

'Well, if you don't mind I'll go up with them,' Sean said.

'Sure,' I replied with more certainty than I felt. 'There's

going to be plenty of people to get me down. Thanks for helping me to here.'

For a few minutes the tent was alive with activity. Then suddenly it emptied.

'Good luck,' I shouted as Sean slipped outside, leaving me alone. Once their voices had faded I was left with only the sound of the wind and flapping fabric for company.

I put on a down jacket and dozed a little, only to be woken around lunchtime by someone bursting into the tent and shouting instructions at me in Russian. I quickly prepared to leave. Outside, I was tied on to a very worn rope with a man whose name was Valeri. I knew very little else about him. Along with the rest of the group, he had been to the summit of the mountain the previous day and was now on his way down.

Valeri set off at a brisk pace down the easy angled snow slopes below the camp to the beginning of the ropes. My ankle seared with pain each time I stumbled and tried to right myself but the Russian barely broke stride and dragged me on through the snow.

We quickly reached the line of ropes. I hoped to have a short rest, but Valeri had other ideas. He simply clipped me to the rope with a karabiner and pointed down. Then Valeri put the rope around his waist and took my weight. I screamed in protest pleading with him to use a belaying device to lower me, but Valeri just looked at me like he was bored. I could understand why. He simply wanted to get off the mountain and now had the additional burden of escorting me down. I would simply have to trust him to lower me with his gloved hands.

The lowers passed in a blur of pain, fear and guilt. I was never comfortable with the manner in which I was being lowered and continually worried about the belays and the rope that was holding me. However, they were putting themselves to a lot of trouble and some danger to help me, so I could hardly complain. The rest of his group quickly caught us up and were forced to wait patiently above while Valeri did his job.

As the afternoon passed, the weather closed in again and it was obvious that we would not get off the mountain until the following day. I had delayed them all. We finally came to the bottom of the ropes in the late afternoon, only to find the enormous snow hole fully occupied. I sat watching helplessly while the Russians levelled a platform and then pitched their tunnel tent in wind and driven snow.

Inside the tent I felt even more inadequate as the Russians smothered me in kindness, making drink after drink and insisting that I ate the best of their remaining food. By western standards most of their clothing and kit was very dated, but they made very good use of limited resources.

During the evening I began to understand something of the communal nature of the Russians' climbing. In some ways this was at odds with the very values that I understood mountaineering to express. I had always been attracted by what I perceived as the feeling of independence it gave, where you used personal climbing and survival skills to achieve a goal you had set yourself in the mountains. In short, there was a large element of self-reliance. This meant that I usually went into the mountains with just one other like-minded climber and felt greater satisfaction when able to operate as a self-contained team of two.

The Russians by contrast relied on sharing many things. People simply slept on shared mats and sleeping bags. They crammed into large tents or snow holes. Some of these actions came about because they did not have access to the resources that we did, but many others underlined a fundamentally different way of thinking. The team we climbed with had even split into two groups as this enabled them to share tents at different camps. By carefully co-ordinating movements of the two parties and where the tents were set up, they could reduce how many tents were carried up and down the mountain. This style of climbing meant the

Russians were carrying smaller loads in their rucksacks than either Sean or I.

In my rage after the accident, I had been ready to dismiss the Russian climbers as reckless and incompetent. It was true they had a different way of doing things in the mountains – a different system. But it was a system that had been carefully thought out and modified through experience. I still thought of some of their practices as unnecessarily dangerous, but some were much more efficient than those that I had learned to be best.

In the morning my ankle felt improved, but it hurt again once I put weight on it. I was lowered a few rope lengths until the angle began to ease and I was able to walk. By transferring as much weight as possible to my ski-poles I could hop along slowly. Fortunately, the soft snow acted as a cushion whenever I put weight on to my damaged foot. Another Russian stayed roped to me, ready to prevent a fall should I step through a snow bridge and into a crevasse.

Eventually, we reached the glacier. When we arrived at a point where there was only bare, hard ice and I was able to see the crevasses that had been hidden higher up by a blanket of snow, the Russian smiled and pointed at my rucksack. I emptied it out on to the ice and put aside some items I would not need. The man packed the gear into his own rucksack, shook my hand and quickly marched off out of view down the glacier. Now I was on my own.

It was a long, lonely and painful walk back to the base camp, but it did give me time to think. The Russians' approach and our own had been quite different, but I imagined their motivation and reasons for climbing were similar to ours. No doubt they enjoyed the physical challenge they found in the mountains and the ingredients of risk and danger certainly added to the undertaking. I felt sure they loved the sublime beauty of the places they visited and relished the elemental contact with their surroundings. In short, I imagined they found the adventure they were seeking in the mountains.

I wondered if they considered their approach to mountaineering to be more or less adventurous than our own. Did they have a different attitude to risk and danger? As I hobbled sadly down the glacier, the thoughts swirled around in my mind and mixed with the throbbing pain from my ankle.

Chapter One

Breaking Free

I looked around the huge sports hall at the hundreds of other students sitting at desks in neat rows an equal distance apart, and sighed. There was still an hour and a half of the examination remaining and I was bored. Sixteen years of education had led up to this point. For many it would be a pinnacle of achievement. I simply felt empty. The years of tests and jumping through academic hoops had left me drained. What had it all been about? And what was it all for? It seemed to me that I had spent the previous three years learning a subject of little interest to me. I remembered the hours spent trying to learn stages in chemical pathways that were part of my course. It had been a mental exercise comparable to memorising ten pages of a telephone directory. Now I could use that knowledge to impress people I did not care to impress, to secure a job I did not want.

I spent much of the remaining time staring out of the small windows into the space outside. Eventually we were told to stop writing, the papers were collected and we were allowed to leave. Outside, I walked on to a playing field and sat with some friends on the grass. It was early summer. The sky was bright and large, diffuse clouds drifted slowly by. The air smelt fresh, earthy and full of life. I breathed in the scents in slow, deliberate breaths and smiled. For the first time I was free from the pressure of doing what other adults deemed best for me. Now, with no commitments or responsibilities, I could do whatever I liked. I had no long-term plans and no idea of how I was going to get by, but a weight had lifted from my shoulders. I sensed the space around me extending into an infinity of possibilities and opportunities. I would climb and I would travel. The world was waiting to be visited and explored. I felt light-headed every time I thought in this way.

When the exam results were published my parents held a small party to celebrate my graduation. All my immediate family and close friends had been invited. For my parents it was a nervous time. They were watching me shun the chance of using my qualification to enter a career profession, for a very uncertain future. However, they were not hostile to what I was doing, but nor were they actively supportive. I felt they were humouring me, hoping that sooner rather than later I would wake up and use my sheet of paper to get a sensible job with a long-term future and a pension.

My grandmother was much more forthright.

'What are you going to do with yourself now Simon?' she asked.

'I'm going to go and climb mountains.'

She looked a little surprised, but not in the slightest bit worried. 'Sounds better than making shoes.'

Her reply puzzled me. I had never really thought of what I was doing in those terms. I climbed because I loved doing it. I had little interest in money or material things, which I saw simply as tools to enable me to climb. My grandmother, having spent much of her working life doing piece-work sewing shoes, had a much less romantic view of the world. To her there was a simple hierarchy when it came to work – professionals had better jobs than factory workers, who had better jobs than labourers. It was encouraging to think that climbing mountains rated highly on her scale, although I wondered if she fully understood the difficulty in making a living from the activity.

*   *   *

'Hey, look at that lot,' said Alan, pointing at people collecting blueberries in the woods around the campsite. 'If they are not careful they could get more than they bargained for.' I burst out laughing. For weeks everyone had been using the area where they were picking berries as a toilet. Although our hygiene standards were low, none of us would have considered taking fruit from around the camp. I was amazed nobody seemed to have noticed the toilet paper.

I looked across the campsite – a small clearing in the pine forest outside Chamonix known as Snell's Field. It had been fuller in July, but now, a week into August, almost two weeks of rain had driven people away. Only the most committed climbers remained. It was hardly surprising. Large sections of the field were under water. Drowned camp fires surrounded by pots, pans, cutlery and discarded food lay abandoned in the mud – a testament to sunny days and outdoor living before the rain had come. Now the social focus had shifted inside larger tents and under polythene shelters that the more industrious had bothered to make. Having lost all faith in the weather, most people were still sitting under the shelters, even though it was the first good morning for days.

The only positive thing about all the waiting was that it had not been expensive. The campsite was free – an illegally occupied piece of waste ground. The only facility was a skip for rubbish provided by the local council. Periodically – no doubt after a rash of complaints – the town gendarmerie would descend on the camp and move everyone along. After a night in the woods or on a nearby official campsite, we would all creep back again. People ate basically, often pooling food and drink in small groups. Many simply shoplifted for food, especially after it became common knowledge that benevolent French laws did not allow prosecution for the offence. The skip provided empty wine bottles that could be returned for their deposits and as the summer progressed supplies swelled further with donations from those who were leaving

Like many camping on the field I had journeyed to Chamonix alone, hoping to meet someone to climb with.

My first pairing of the season had not been too successful. I had met Jamal, whom I knew and had climbed with a little at college. After barely starting our chosen climb – The Frendo Spur on the Aiguille du Midi – Jamal slipped, fell a short distance and badly hurt his ankle. It took the rest of the day to retreat down to the base of the route and retrace the short walk back to the Midi Plan cable-car station. Jamal paid for a ride back down into Chamonix, while to save money I walked back down into the valley through the forest. By the time I arrived back in town, an X-ray in the hospital had confirmed what we both suspected – Jamal's ankle was broken and his climbing season over. He caught a coach back home a couple of days later.

Partnerships were usually forged around a stove or camp fire after several bottles of shared cheap red wine. This was how I had met Alan Wilkie, a New Zealander, who like many Antipodean climbers was broadening his horizons and experience by visiting Europe. We had agreed to climb together as soon as the next suitable spell of weather came along.

A few days later Alan and I caught the last cable car of the day from the village of Argentière up to the Col des Grands Montets. From the cable-car station we had the luxury of walking down for most of the approach. As the last sunlight touched the mountain tops we reached the Argentière Glacier, crossed to its far side, and walked gently uphill a short distance to a large climbing hut bearing the same name. Having bought cable-car tickets, we decided against further expense and settled down in our sleeping bags on a terrace cut into the hillside outside the hut. Directly opposite the hut on the other side of the glacier stood the mountain we had come to climb.

The North-East spur of Les Droites would present us with a challenge, especially after the inactivity of the previous weeks. In the gathering darkness I could make out the shapely profile of the spur, which ran right to the summit. The most difficult climbing would be low down, as the spur dropped away steeply to the glacier forming a large rock buttress.

To climbers some features on mountains appear elegant and compelling ways of reaching the summit. The route we had chosen was such an objective.

I lay in my sleeping bag, looking at the stars forming in the darkening sky and feeling nervous and apprehensive, but at the same time excited. The feeling of freedom and uncertainty was intoxicating, completely the opposite of the stifled oppression I had felt just a few weeks earlier. Here in the mountains I could operate within a much looser set of unwritten rules, which were formulated by my contemporaries and which changed over time as new techniques developed and others became out-dated. These mountaineering ethics are hotly debated in climbing circles as they vary regionally and nationally and even between different individuals. Within this framework climbers set their own standards and if they end up using techniques or practices they themselves consider unethical they know that they have climbed in bad style. However, compared to more formal sports, with their extensive rules and regulations, along with referees and judges to enforce them, mountaineering seems free and anarchic. Personally, while climbing I feel only accountable to myself and whoever I chose to climb with.

It was difficult to sleep much, as after about midnight others started leaving the hut. These 'Alpine Starts', as they are known, are often used by climbers in mountains as glaciers and snow slopes can be crossed while still frozen and then the climb and descent completed during the day.

We slipped away just before dawn. It did not take long to prepare to leave, as we had left the stove back at the campsite. 'We'll find plenty to drink on the way,' Alan had convinced me. The walk across the glacier did not take long and we soon stood beneath the climb. After putting on rock boots and stowing our large plastic mountaineering boots in our rucksacks, we began.

The bottom of the spur was slabby, and I raced up the first rope-length of the climb. The slabs soon led into a series of grooves and then steepened further into corners and cracks.

After a slow, shaky start in the cold of early morning, our hands and bodies gradually began to warm and we gained momentum.

The climbing was of sufficient difficulty to make it interesting, but never too hard to interrupt our progress and we encountered none of the loose or shattered rock which blights some Alpine climbs. The day slid by in a blur of rapid movement and by early evening we had finished climbing the steep rocky buttress that formed the lower half of the route. Suddenly, we burst from the shadow into bright afternoon sun. The climbing became easier, but more time-consuming as we were now following a ridge that was broken with pinnacles. We weaved round them on their easier sides. We were both moving quickly, but I was puzzled why Alan kept stopping and dropping to his knees. It seemed as if he was looking for something.

'How about spending the night here?' Alan asked when I joined him on a large flat platform as the light was starting to fade.

'Seems fine,' I replied beginning to prepare for the bivouac. 'I don't know about you, but I could do with a brew.'

'Haven't you been getting water as we've gone along?'

'Where from?'

'If you look carefully you can find small dribbles running all over the place, especially since we've been in the sun.' Alan produced a thin piece of rubber pipe, pushed it into a crack on the wall of rock behind the bivouac and sucked at a dribble of water. 'I always carry one of these,' he added waving the pipe around. 'Don't you?'

I shook my head, feeling rather stupid. The water bottle I had filled at the hut was now nearly empty. It was becoming obvious that unless I was careful I was going to be very dehydrated.

We settled down for the night on the ledge. Alan had arranged our food. He pulled out a cake and a block of butter, cut thick slices of each and handed me a slice of cake-butter sandwich.

'There is more energy in fat than any other food,' he explained, 'and it makes the cake easier to eat.'

'Right,' I replied, unconvinced.

Alan's ideas on eating and drinking in the mountains were certainly unconventional. The cake did go down well, but I managed to melt precious little snow inside my water bottle. Wherever I put the bottle it drew heat from my body, making me feel cold, and I had to continually refill it with snow. The meagre drops of fluid produced hardly seemed worth the effort.

I woke feeling parched, but not too concerned. The ground above looked reasonable – large sections of snow and ice dotted with small rock buttresses – and I reasoned that we would be able to climb quicker using the plastic boots, crampons and ice-axes that we had carried in our rucksacks on the first day. Hopefully, I would be able to find water using Alan's technique, but even if this was not the case I reckoned we would easily reach the top and descend to the hut on the other side during the day.

We began slowly and got slower. The sun hit us very early in the morning and it soon became unbearably hot. My mouth became drier and however closely I examined the rocks around me I could find no water. Whenever Alan followed he would arrive at my stance and tell me about the puddles I had missed on the way. The slabs of cake and butter we ate occasionally did little to slake my thirst and as time went by Alan began to suffer as well. Afternoon clouds rolled in and I began to get worried a storm was approaching.

'Let's try moving together,' I suggested, hoping we would move faster.

'Don't be stupid. We don't want to blow it now,' came the blunt reply.

It was a reasonable point – climbing together even when roped is not as safe as climbing individually, when the non-climbing partner can belay the other from a secure anchor. Sometimes when moving together there are no anchors at all and the pair rely on the possibility of the rope snagging in the event of a fall as the only means of protection. When we finally started following a gently angled snow ridge to the summit it was very late in the day.

We stood on the top and watched the sun setting to the west. It was a fantastic sight, but we knew we were in for an unplanned extra night. After descending a little way we found a flat area on the ridge protected by a few rocks. We scooped two trenches in the snow, put our sleeping mats and bags in them and settled down for the night.

I was desperately thirsty, but my water bottle yielded only a few drops of melted snow. We ate some more cake and butter and tried to sleep. The night passed very slowly. It was bitterly cold and I cursed my thin, inadequate sleeping bag. Eventually the sun rose, but it was some time before it was warm enough to leave.

We followed the ridge along for a short way before dropping down to a col, where a couloir led down the south side of the mountain. After rigging up the ropes we abseiled down into it. Once off the summit ridge and out of the wind, it became hot again. Sweat started to pour from our already dehydrated bodies. Lumps of dried saliva formed in my mouth and throat and painful cracks opened on my lips. Pulling the heavy ropes down after each abseil was increasingly tiring and the harder we worked, the more we sweated.

Finally we reached a snow slope that led down on to the glacier, but the sun had already turned the snow to mush. We staggered down the slope and across the glacier sinking up to our knees, while trying to knock clods of wet snow from our feet that stuck to them with every step. Eventually we reached a rocky moraine ridge. A little further down was a small stream. We stopped and drank the ice-cold glacial water until our stomachs were painfully full.

'Cheers,' I said, shaking Alan's hand. 'It was a good route, but I'm not going on a climb like that again without a stove.'

Alan grinned, looking a little guilty, then picked up his pack and began the long walk back to the campsite in Chamonix.

*   *   *

'Watch me!' came the cry from above. I had been huddled on a small ledge for what seemed like hours, patiently paying out rope as John Silvester climbed above. The climbing was difficult and his progress slow. My attention had drifted and now a large loop of slack hung below me. I quickly pulled the slack rope back through the belay device, hoping John would not fall. Then the rope came tight. Moments later I heard a metallic clattering sound, interrupted by muffled thuds. John suddenly cleared a small overhang above and came to a stop, as I was pulled upwards off my stance by the force of his fall. For a few moments there was silence, then, aware that the crisis was over, I relaxed and let out a sigh. John's distinctive high-pitched laugh drifted down. He was unhurt.

John and I were spending our second day climbing the Croz Spur on the North Face of Les Grandes Jorasses. On my first visit to the Alps the year before I had climbed the nearby Walker Spur. Looking at the Walker Spur as we climbed memories came drifting back. I recalled pulling off a flake of rock low down on the climb, which narrowly missed a party climbing just below. I had managed to lose both my head-torch and one of my axes during the ascent and once the climb was completed I had hobbled down the far side of the mountain into Italy, my feet blistered with trench foot as I had forgotten to remove my plastic boots during the two nights spent on the mountain. However, I soon forgot my mistakes, the fear and the suffering and recalled the joy of moving through such terrain with the sun setting behind distant peaks, and the sense of achievement once the climb was complete. The memories of the experience had stayed with me through my last year at college and inspired a second visit. Now, on our second day of climbing, we were perhaps two-thirds way up the 1,000 metre route. John's fall simply confirmed that the climbing was harder than we expected. I had suffered a similar tumble earlier in the day.

John lived in North Wales in one of the largest climbing communities in Britain. I liked his relaxed manner and our friendship had grown in the campsite through the summer over breakfast pancakes and evening fires. For most of the season, guiding work had prevented him from climbing much for himself. However, once it became clear that we both shared an ambition to climb the Croz, we made arrangements to climb together as soon as John's work commitments were finished.

The rope started to inch upwards again. The fall was more of an inconvenience to John than a worry. He quickly regained his high point and was now making progress again. I began to daydream again. The view down the Leschaux Glacier and the Mer de Glace was hypnotic. A shout floated down, the rope pulled tight at my waist and I started to follow.

Once above the overhang I reached the point where John had fallen. The difficulties were similar to those that had been slowing us all along. Thin layers of crusty snow lay over rock. Sometimes it was easier to drop ice-axes, let them hang by their wrist loops and use hand-holds brushed clear of snow to make upward progress. At other times the ice was deep enough to accept axe placements, or else they could be placed in cracks in the rock and hauled on. This absorbing style is known as mixed climbing. Unfortunately, clearing away loose ice and snow and deciding how to execute each series of moves was time-consuming. With the snow brushed clear, it was much easier to see what was needed to be done. I repeated the moves John had fallen from, relying on very insecure axe placements in just millimetres of ice. It was easy to see how his axes had simply ripped from the thin ice, precipitating his tumble.

A large, reasonably angled icefield stretched above. John handed me the gear and I carried on. After the difficulties below it was nice to be moving freely again. A simple matter of planting one axe above the other in the ice and then skipping up on cramponed boots. After climbing half a rope-length I paused, wound a hollow screw into the ice, clipped the rope to it and continued. The ice-screw would lessen my fall in the unlikely event of a slip.

'You might as well start climbing,' I shouted down to

John confidently, when nearly all the rope was used up. He dismantled the belay and began to follow. Now we were climbing together with only the single ice-screw to protect us both should we fall.

We made steady progress and by early evening were at the top of the icefield. I banged a piton into a crack in the first rock I reached and clipped myself to it. It was nice to have the security of a rock anchor again. While climbing the ice there was always a nagging doubt about how good the ice-screw anchors were, as it was impossible to judge the strength of the ice itself. There were no such doubts hanging from a metal peg hammered into clean, hard, rock.

A little higher a steep headwall reared up, forming the upper part of the mountain. Already the sun was setting and lengthening shadows of the surrounding peaks were stretching across the glaciers below. It was obvious there was not enough of the day left to climb the headwall, so I started to look around for somewhere to spend the night. John climbed steadily up towards me.

Then suddenly, just a few metres below me, John's feet slipped and both axes popped out of their shallow placements. A look of surprise and terror shot across his face. My heart leapt. As I was still looking for more anchors, I was not belaying him. I had not even begun to take in the slack rope between us. I expected him to simply fall and cart-wheel off down the ice and was puzzled when he did not. Instead his axes and crampons simply slid down the ice, sounding like fingernails being dragged down a blackboard. As he accelerated away from me the pitch of the sound increased. I was sure that any moment he would sever contact with the ice, but he did not. Then he jerked to an abrupt halt, somehow still glued to the mountain. It seemed his crampon points had lodged in a faint fracture line in the ice and somehow stopped his fall. He calmly swung his axes back into the ice and looked up.

'You lucky sod!' I shouted down.

A smile spread nervously over John's face, followed by his

usual high-pitched laughter. Had the fall continued he would have gone nearly the whole fifty-metre rope length and tested the single metal piton to which I was anchored.

We found a ledge at the foot of the headwall that was just about big enough for us both to lie on and settled down for the night. While the stove roared, we watched the valleys darken as the mountains went golden in the evening light. The party below were still struggling and their lead climber fell close to where John had tumbled earlier in the day.

'They're not going to have a very comfortable night,' John said, his laughter echoing from the headwall above. It looked like they were heading for a poor bivouac at the bottom of the snow-field.

The night was not comfortable for me either. Having bought a down jacket from an impoverished Polish climber on the campsite, I had felt it would be a good idea to take it rather than the sleeping bag I had found so cold on the previous climb. But I realised my error the evening before. The jacket was good and kept my upper body warm, but my legs and feet, protected only by my empty rucksack, were freezing. It was another unsuccessful experiment that I vowed never to repeat.

That night it snowed, as it had done on our previous night on the face. I slept fitfully between bouts of shivering and occasionally looked enviously across at John curled up asleep in his sleeping bag.

Breakfast was a sombre affair. I was still very cold, but the snow had stopped. We agreed to move right and join a thin gully that cut up to the summit ridge rather than to try and breach the headwall direct.

John led off and I followed him across a series of rocky slabs dusted in snow to a belay at the bottom of a steep open corner.

'Looks difficult,' John said with a smile, handing me the equipment. I set off, reached the corner and stopped. The rock became soft and smooth. I placed a poor peg, clipped the rope to it and began to move upwards. A thin ribbon of hard, black ice seemed to offer the only hope of getting higher. It took several blows of the ice-axe just to make a single placement. I pulled up and hacked another placement above, but it felt bunched and clumsy placing one axe above the other. My feet skidded ineffectually on the smooth rock, the axes jumped from the ice and I fell. The peg held and I bounced around on the rope just above John.

'You have a go,' I said. 'I don't have a clue how to do that.'

We changed round and John was soon tackling the corner. John was affectionately nicknamed Skeletor, because of his bony frame. However, he was far from weak. I could only admire his superior strength and technique as he somehow inched up the ribbon of ice, his legs bridged wide apart with crampons resting on the smallest of edges in the rock. Twice his feet slipped and for a few seconds it looked as if he might fall as he desperately scrabbled to get them back into position, but he was strong enough to hang from his axes. Somehow he maintained contact with the mountain and upward movement. After about ten metres he let out a shriek of delight.

'There's an easy gully to the top from here.'

I struggled to follow the steep corner and felt sure I would have fallen had John not been providing tight rope from the belay above.

Leading the following pitch I began to relax and enjoy our position. Only a handful of mountains were above us now and the indifferent weather that had troubled us lower down the mountain had finally cleared.

At the next belay, with John climbing above, I watched the pair of climbers below us. They were now only about 100 metres lower, having gained ground on us while we struggled to climb the steep corner. I could clearly see the leader trying to work out a sequence of moves up the thin ribbon of ice. His actions looked full of the indecision of a climber having difficulties. My attempt to climb the same ground would have looked similar. He was trying one axe placement, then another, stepping up a move and then back down again. Then he fell, peeling off backwards with his limbs held out like a skydiver.

'Quite an impressive lob,' I thought to myself as the second climber was pulled from his stance. 'This is wrong,' I told myself a moment later, 'something will stop their fall in a minute.' But nothing did. The men started to scream as they gathered speed. Their rucksacks burst, scattering stoves, pans, food and clothing on each impact. Then they disappeared from my sight over steeper ground into the upper part of the icefield. I expected them to reappear, but they did not. There was silence. I felt physically sick.

Minutes passed. I was just beginning to think about what we could do to help, when I heard loud animal-like groans. Down at the top of the icefield one of the climbers slid slowly into my view and then gradually accelerated down the icy slope. Then the second climber appeared, pulled along behind by the taut rope. The rope must have snagged near the top of the icefield, temporarily halting their fall. Now, for whatever reason, the rope had freed. I watched them slither down the ice, but turned away as the first climber plunged off the bottom of it. I had seen enough. In all likelihood the men would go the entire length of the 1,000-metre face.

'Those guys below have fallen,' I told John as I joined him at the stance above.

'Are they okay?'

'I doubt it. They've gone all the way.'

'You're kidding.' John looked at me, wanting my story to be a joke. I shook my head. For once there was no manic laughter. Now John was silent.

Later John kept on talking about the accident as we climbed the last pitch to the summit ridge and started abseiling down the other side. It was as if he still did not believe what I had told him. I felt numb and unable to think properly. On the first abseil of the descent I failed to stop at the end of the ropes and went straight off the end of them. Fortunately, I was on easy ground and simply rolled over backwards, to be halted by the deep, wet snow.

After the abseils we crossed a small glacier and walked demoralised down a rocky ridge to the Grandes Jorasses hut. Inside we told our sad story to the warden, who calmly radioed down to the authorities, before kindly making us some cups of tea. The joy of the climb and the feeling of achievement had been completely obliterated by the accident.

A few days later, back in Chamonix, a group of Japanese climbers arrived at my tent. They were friends of the climbers that had been below us on the Croz. It had taken them a long time to find us. The only information they had was that the accident had been reported by two British climbers. Through a very broken conversation in simple English, John and I were able to tell them what had happened to their friends. From what I had seen, I could only assume that the anchors of their belay had been inadequate. They may have been poorly placed, or perhaps they had relied on just a single anchor. Whatever the reason, the belay had been unable to hold the weight of the initial fall and once it had failed, there was little hope for either climber.

The Japanese climbers had been unlucky. It is very rare that a set of belay anchors are tested by a fall directly on to them. Normally, the rope would be clipped through a piece of protection above. If they had done so, the higher anchor would have held the fall, and even if the piece of equipment had ripped it would have dampened some of the fall's energy, lessening the load which ultimately reached the belay.

John and I had managed to assemble a very secure belay with no less than three separate pieces of equipment placed in cracks in the rock that had been painstakingly cleared of snow. Both John and I took it as a rule that a belay required at least two anchors, preferably three. The only time we abandoned this rule was when only a single anchor could be found. I wondered what the Japanese climbers had done. Had they been following a similar rule and simply been hasty constructing that single belay in their rush to get to the top, or had they been following a set of personal rules with less of a safety margin than ours?

For us, the climb had been a demanding challenge that had stretched us to the limits of our climbing abilities. It had been an adventure. For the Japanese climbers the same challenge had been a disaster.

John had to return to England after the Croz climb and I began to cast around for another climbing partner. One wet evening in the Brasserie National I struck up a conversation with a climber I had not met before. It quickly became clear that he had done a fair number of difficult Alpine climbs and that we shared some common friends. The pieces in the mental jigsaw I was building up fell into place when he told me his name was Joe Simpson.

Joe was a legend in mountaineering circles, primarily because he was still living, after two very serious accidents in the mountains above Chamonix. Once he had been avalanched down the summit slopes of Les Courtes and had fallen 1,000 metres down its North Face, only to walk away with injuries no more serious than a few cuts and bruises. On another occasion a bivouac ledge half way up the Bonatti Pillar on Les Dru had collapsed beneath him and a sleeping friend leaving them hanging from a single metal peg. They then spent a nerve-racking twelve hours suspended from the peg before they were rescued by helicopter. That he had survived either of the accidents was surprising, but to survive both was nothing short of miraculous.

Some friends from Sheffield had spent time sharing a flat with Joe in Chamonix two winters earlier. I remembered they had given him the nick-name Captain Scarlet because he was indestructible. With his dark brown hair and square jaw the name now seemed even more appropriate.

He was smaller than I expected, but obviously strong and determined and had an engaging way of talking to people. I found him to be very good company.

'Would you like to do a route with me?' he asked towards the end of the evening.

'Yeah. What have you got in mind?'

'The Cecchinel Nominé.'

'That would be great.'

The climb had been a longstanding ambition of mine. It was an elegant ice-climb following thin gullies and ramps on the Eckpfeiler Buttress on the south side of Mont Blanc. The route had the added bonus of joining the Peuterey Ridge at its top. We would be able to continue up this ridge to the summit of Mont Blanc – the highest peak in the European Alps.

Two days later we caught a cable car to the summit of the Aiguille du Midi and spent a tiring day of glacier walking to reach the Trident Hut overlooking the Brenva Glacier. The Eckpfeiler Buttress lay at the head of the glacier. It was a perfect evening and we sat outside the hut eating slices of cured ham and tinned pineapple discussing where the route went. Joe's eating tastes were much more to my liking than Alan's.

We paid for a night in the hut and were woken very early by the clamour of people trying to leave. By the time we left, flickering head torches formed a string of light up the lower sections of two popular climbs on Mont Blanc – Route Major and the Brenva Ridge.

The morning silence was regularly broken by the sickening sound of falling rocks, followed by hysterical yelling. The highest climbers were knocking rocks on those lower down, who then shouted up hoping to stop the bombardment. It was a horrible scene to witness, as it was possible to follow some of the larger rocks by the sparks they emitted each time they bounced. Whenever the sparks and head-torch flashes came close together I expected to hear a blood-curdling scream as someone was hit.

I felt relieved. We would be on a different route and not have to join the deadly human traffic jam above. Even so, we would still have to cross a couloir at the base of the two routes, into which much of the falling debris was funnelling.

We left the hut in silence. Joe went in front and it was my job to keep the rope tight between us by altering the pace as I followed him. The rope would offer protection should either of us fall into a crevasse, and if it was tight such a fall would be shorter.

We had not been going long when one of my crampons fell off.

'Hold on Joe,' I shouted, as I struggled to strap it back on to the boot. Eventually it did so, but somehow it did not seem to fit properly. It was hard to understand why as I had been using the crampons all season without any problems.

We soon reached the bottom of the snow slope and crossed on to the glacier. We had not been on the glacier long before there was a muffled yell and the rope tugged at my waist. I lifted my head and in the far reach of my torch beam I could just make out the upper part of Joe's body above the snow. The rest was below. He had fallen into a crevasse. I pushed my ice-axe into the snow, and braced myself to prevent him falling any further into the slot in the ice.

'Don't worry,' Joe called. 'It's not a deep one.'

After a lot of wriggling he managed to haul himself out of the hole, but did not get up.

'What's the matter?' I asked, walking towards him.

'I've spiked myself.'

When I reached Joe he was looking at his leg. There was a hole in his left calf. His crampon had obviously caught the leg during the short fall into the crevasse. Thick, dark blood was already oozing from the wound.

'Are you going to be all right to carry on?'

'I should be, but I'm sure it's going to stiffen up later.'

We started moving again, but after a few steps my progress was being hampered. I looked down at my boots.

'Shit. Hold on Joe. My crampon's fallen off again.'

I sensed the delays were starting to eat away at our momentum and motivation. However, we soon reached the couloir down which climbers had been kicking debris. We raced across the section of glacier littered in rocks and luckily the mountain remained silent. After we had cleared the danger zone my crampon fell off again. It was now almost light.

'What do you think we should do?' I asked.

'I don't think we have time to do our route now. What about another?'

We sat down in the snow on our rucksacks and I pulled out the guide book. We studied it intently.

'How about this?' Joe said, pointing at a route on the North Face of the Aiguille Blanche de Peuterey. The mountain was close, being just beyond the buttress we had originally planned on climbing. 'Fairly straightforward ice-climbing, and we can continue up the Peuterey Ridge afterwards to the top of Mont Blanc.'

'Better than nothing I suppose,' I replied, not wanting to return to Chamonix empty-handed. After all, we had paid a cable car fare and the weather forecast was good for the following few days.

As we set off again I studied our new climb. Essentially it was a large icefield, at about a 45-degree angle. At half way there was a thin band of rock, cut by a gully which was going to give the hardest climbing. But overall it looked straightforward, if a little exposed. We soon reached the bottom of the climb.

'Shall we rope up, Joe?'

'There doesn't seem much point, unless we pitch the whole route.'

Joe was right. If we climbed roped together over such ground without belays it would mean that if one fell the other would be pulled off as well. Climbing unroped would simply mean one death instead of two under such circumstances. I led off, after first taking the precaution of clipping an ice-screw to my harness. If I did get into trouble, I would at least be able to place the screw in the ice and clip myself to it.

The screw was not needed. It was simply a case of swinging one ice-axe then the other and kicking a little higher with both feet. The axes and crampons held perfectly in good plastic-like ice. The only problem was the strain on over-used calf muscles, as we balanced our entire weight on the front, forward-facing points of our crampons. With rucksacks laden with rope and enough equipment to tackle a difficult technical climb, the calves reached a point where they felt like they were burning. Then it was necessary to chop a small horizontal ledge in the ice with the axe and stand on it. If we swapped feet and shook the free leg, the pain subsided enough to continue.

The climbing was fast and exhilarating. Soon the sun came up over a bank of cloud in the valleys of Italy below, adding to the feeling of exposure. It felt wonderful to be climbing so speedily, free of ropes and the clutter of equipment high above the clouds. All too quickly we were on the summit of the mountain, and we made a short descent down a snow slope to the Col de Peuterey. Amazingly, the crampon that fell from my boot walking across the flat glacier at the start of the day had stayed attached while being kicked into hard ice on the climb.

When we arrived at the col, it was still only early morning. The amphitheatre of ice and snow, high on the south side of Mont Blanc, was stunning and it seemed fitting that having made the effort to get to such a remote place we were rewarded with the incredible beauty all around.

We pulled out the stove, lit it and put on a pan of snow to melt. Soon it was incredibly hot. It seemed as if the snow and ice were reflecting and concentrating the heat on to the basin where we sat. I began to feel lethargic.

'Come on Joe,' I said, after a brew and a bite to eat. 'We'd better get going. There's still an awful long way to the top.' A snow slope led up out of the basin to a long meandering snow ridge. The summit was way out of sight. Our plan was to reach the top and drop a good way down the French side of the mountain to spend the night.

Climbing out of the basin was difficult from the start. The heat was stifling and the snow was now melting and very soft. With each step we sank up to our knees. Joe had been very quiet while we were at the col and now he began to lag behind.

'I don't feel so good,' he gasped, slumping over his ice-axe for support. 'Can't seem to breathe properly.'

'You don't look too good either.'

We carried on, but progress became ever slower. Joe's breathing became faster, but was increasingly shallow. I had no idea of what was wrong or how to help him. All I could do was wait and offer encouragement. The morning slipped by. By the middle of the afternoon I began to get seriously worried. What was I going to do? Would Joe have to be rescued? Where were we going to spend the night? There had been climbers around us earlier, but now we were alone.

'Have to sit down,' Joe said, as we reached some broken ground that led up to the beginning of the snow ridge. He slumped on to a rocky ledge and promptly lost consciousness. I made him as comfortable as possible, but there was little I could do. His breathing seemed more relaxed and deeper. I got into my sleeping bag and sat nervously eating sweets. A whole kilogramme passed my lips before Joe came to his senses.

'Better spend the night here,' he said, promptly falling asleep again.

Later, I made some hot drinks and food and woke Joe to share them. He seemed better and we talked a little before he drifted off to sleep again. For me sleep was much more difficult. I was worried about what the morning would bring. The whole situation was out of the realms of my mountaineering experience. It was the lack of control I disliked more than anything else. I had been in tight spots in the mountains before, but had always been in a position to do something about the situation.

'How are you feeling?' I asked, first thing in the morning.

'A lot better. But I'm still worried.'

'Why's that?'

'Well. What happens if I end up feeling like I did yesterday on the snow ridge above? There's nowhere to stop safely. I could fall off and if we're roped together you'd be off as well.'

Joe had a point. The snow ridge above was smooth and steep. An ice-axe planted in the snow was likely to be the best belay we would get. If Joe's condition returned while we climbed the ridge we could have some very serious problems.

'So what are we going to do?' I asked.

'Get rescued,' Joe replied matter of factly.

'And how do we do that?'

'We wait for those people coming up and then ask them to call a chopper once they get to the hut on the French side of the mountain.'

'Oh. Right,' I said, hardly believing what I was hearing, but willing to bow to Joe's experience in these matters. After all, he had been rescued by helicopter before.

It was still dark and we sat in our sleeping bags watching three torch lights moving slowly up the snow slope below. By the time they joined us it was dawn. It felt strange as the men arrived. We were barely out of our sleeping bags and they had obviously been on the go for hours. Joe stood up and introduced himself to the three Frenchmen. They did not look very impressed. My own limited knowledge of French meant I could not really understand their conversation, but Joe was getting more and more agitated. There was a loud final exchange of words and the men left.

'Would you believe it,' Joe fumed. 'They called us lazy and won't ask for a chopper.'

'I guess we'll have to get ourselves out of here then,' I replied.

I kept quiet and tried to hide my amusement as Joe continued to complain about the Frenchmen's behaviour. Then we agreed it would be easier and safer if I carried the spare rope and some extra communal kit. Joe was less likely to get a recurrence of the previous day's condition carrying a smaller load and if he did get into trouble again, it would be easier to manage if we were less weighed down.

Once the repacking was complete, we set off. We made steady progress to the top of the ridge and by late morning reached a plateau. As we plodded slowly across the gently angled slopes towards the summit of Mont Blanc, I was aware that Joe was now going stronger than I was. He had obviously made a full recovery. Later, after talking with others, we concluded that he had probably suffered from heat stroke and dehydration. A decent night's rest and some drinks had been all that was needed to cure the condition.

On the summit of Mont Blanc we stopped, shook hands and took some photographs. It had turned out well in the end. Although we had not achieved what we set out to do, we had overcome a lot of difficulties to complete a long and elegant climb.

Back in the bar that night we celebrated our minor success. My time in Chamonix had been a roller-coaster of experiences and emotions. On my first visit the previous year, my inexperience had meant that almost every climb turned into an ordeal. It was only months later that I was able to view what had happened objectively, conclude that I enjoyed alpinism and decide to return. Now I was starting to get more from the effort I put in and felt comfortable enough with my surroundings to enjoy myself at the time rather than retrospectively. More importantly, my growing experience and confidence allowed me to try out different ways of doing things, to improvise when confronted by new or difficult situations and not to repeat previous mistakes. By putting myself in such extreme situations I was quickly learning the skills required of an alpinist, but I also sensed I was learning a lot about myself as a person – the levels of joy and sadness I could reach, how strong my body was and how it operated when tired to the point of exhaustion, how I reacted in intensely stressful situations and how I dealt with others under such circumstances and a whole host of other sides to my personality. After all the years of formal education, which had sapped my spirit and numbed my mind, it felt like I was actually starting to learn again. However, above all else I had tasted freedom. I sensed that along with the like-minded people I had met during the summer I had cast aside some of our society's petty rules and behaviour. As a result life felt like the big adventure I imagined it should be – unpredictable, spontaneous, risky and above all fun.

Joe and I talked all evening. He knew a number of climbers in Sheffield who were also friends of mine and had spent the previous winter sharing an apartment and a cleaning job with them in Chamonix. In the recession of the early 1980s many unemployed climbers had drifted into Sheffield, lured by the city's closeness to the Peak District and the cheap, subsidised public transport that gave access to it. Joe had decided to join that swelling army of unemployed climbers. We were going to be neighbours, near enough. Over the course of the night it became obvious that we shared some ideas and ambitions.

'I've been thinking about going to Peru next summer,' Joe said suggestively.

'I'd be interested in that,' I replied.

Chapter Two

Peaks and Troughs

I sat in the chair looking nervously round the bank foyer. In the week since I returned from Peru I had managed to avoid such places. Now I remembered what I disliked about them – the solemn, oppressive atmosphere and the screens of glass shielding the expressionless cashiers. Then there were the customers who always seemed to behave as if they had entered a church, dropping their voices to a whisper, adopting an almost reverential manner and then looking pleasantly surprised when handed some of their own money, as if they expected not to be allowed any.

The previous weeks had been a roller-coaster of experiences and emotions. There had almost been too much to absorb and learn, and at times I felt as if I was being overwhelmed by what was happening. I had been barely able to cope.

Joe and I had managed to overcome the initial difficulties posed by travelling to remote mountain regions at high altitude and to complete a fine new route on the West Face of Siula Grande in the Peruvian Andes. Unfortunately, Joe had fallen and broken his leg on the descent. From then on our retreat from the mountain became a protracted struggle, from which Joe was lucky to escape with his life.

Joe would later write about our experiences in his book *Touching the Void*, but on our return he had been admitted to hospital to supplement treatment he had received in Peru. I returned to Sheffield and in a whirlwind of socialising broke the news of our incredible adventure to our friends. It felt as if my body had been pumped high with adrenalin ever since Joe's accident. Entering the bank was my most sobering experience in weeks.

'The manager is ready to see you now, Mr Yates.' A woman cashier directed me towards a small office to one side of the main banking area. He greeted me with a very formal handshake.

'Take a seat Mr Yates,' he said, pointing towards a table with two small plastic chairs on the nearest side and a large leather chair on the other. I walked round the table and sat down in the leather chair.

The bank manager looked at me like a teacher disciplining a disruptive child.

'Round the other side of the table, please, Mr Yates.'

He began a polite chat, asking how I spent my time and about our trip to Peru. Just as he was beginning to seem human, the inevitable happened.

'What about this?' he asked, waving a letter written by Sean Smith in front of my face. Reality hit me like a brick. I remembered why I had been called to the bank in the first place. When it had been time to leave for Peru I was several hundred pounds short of the money I needed. My winter in Sheffield since returning from the Alps the previous autumn had been spent surviving on unemployment benefit and a few odd jobs. It had not produced the desired surplus of money I had dreamily expected. Unsurprisingly, the bank refused a loan. In a carefully calculated operation I had moved around different cash machines in Sheffield one afternoon and simply withdrawn the cash. I had left for Peru by the time the letters started arriving at my vacated flat. My friend Sean, who occupied another flat in the same house, had sent a letter denying that I even lived at the address. Rather than throwing them off my trail, the letter simply incensed the bank who then traced and contacted my parents. My embarrassed mother and father had promised that I would come in to the bank as soon as I returned. I mumbled an inadequate reply.

'And how do you intend to pay back the money you owe us Mr Yates?'

'Well, I've got a hundred pounds here and I'm picking strawberries at the moment.' I had been helping an old farmer friend of the family for a few days. 'And I'm sure something else will come up.'

The bank manager gave me his teacher look again.

'Well Mr Yates, I think you've had your fun. I suggest you settle down, get a good job and pay us back our money.'

I agreed to start paying back my debt a little each week and left. I had wanted to scream at the man and the bank he represented. They seemed to stand for everything I hated, everything that was reduced to its rightful insignificance once I was in the mountains: authority, arrogance, rules and pettiness. In short, the man and his bank stood for a system where a set of blanket rules and regulations are applied to a myriad of different individuals. I had wanted to borrow a very modest amount of money to go and climb a mountain, a venture no doubt viewed by the bank as unusual and risky and unlikely to produce any return on their investment. Yet the same bank was happy to use its customers' money to gamble on stock and currency markets, or lend to businesses or developing countries that had no hope of ever paying back the loans. I had wanted to shout at the bank manager, 'What about passion? What about about freedom? What about adventure?', but I would have been wasting my breath. The man and the bank he worked for viewed life in terms of pounds, pence and rules. I was viewed very dimly because I had broken their rules and I still owed the bank money.

The story of our close escape in Peru was doing the rounds of the climbing communities by word of mouth by the time Joe returned to Sheffield. I found the modest attention we were receiving in the climbing world a little embarrassing. Joe seemed much more comfortable and agreed to write an article about our adventures for the climbing magazine *High*.

The editor, Geoff Birtles, offered me some money to write my side of the story, but I wanted to look forward rather than dwell on a painful experience that was now in the past, and I felt shy and rather self-conscious about putting my thoughts down on paper. I had heard of, and even witnessed lives being lost in the mountains, but somehow the events had always seemed a little distant, somehow removed from my own life. What had happened in Peru was very immediate and very real. I was now truly aware of the ultimate penalty that mountaineering could exact, but at the same time my desire to climb was undiminished.

A national newspaper somehow got to hear of what had happened and contacted Joe, offering to buy the story. When Joe told a friend, Neil Buttle, about the offer, he saw an opportunity for a joke. Neil got a friend to telephone Joe pretending to be a journalist from a rival newspaper, offering more money for the story. Joe suspected nothing and promptly told the first journalist about the higher offer. On the back of the prank bid, they upped their offer and we accepted.

I could hardly believe our luck. There was enough money to pay off my debts and even some left over. But although the newspaper article solved my immediate financial problems, it also brought a lot more attention. We were interviewed for a local television programme. People I barely knew wanted to talk to me about what had happened. 'Are you going to carry on climbing?' many would ask. They spoke to me in gentle sympathetic tones, as if they expected me to be seriously mentally scarred by the experience. The continual fuss and questioning quickly began to annoy me.

The idea of giving up climbing had never entered my head, even in the darkest moments in Peru. Joe had been through much more of an ordeal. He had nearly died, and although he had come back from the edge, the experience had deeply disturbed him. It would take him some time to get over the mental trauma of what he had been through. In addition, his badly injured knee was a continuing physical reminder of what had happened. The doctors were saying Joe would be left with a permanent limp and unable to climb again. I had got away with a few frostbitten fingers which had quickly healed.

Overall our adventure had been exhilarating and exciting, beyond my wildest expectations. At first I had enjoyed sharing some of that excitement and magic and the awe of what had been a life-altering experience, with friends and family. Now it seemed as if everybody wanted a piece of our adventure, as if hearing about it was acting as a substitute for the lack of excitement in their own lives. I knew exactly what I wanted. John Silvester and some other friends were out in the French Alps. After a little over a month back in Britain I booked a coach ticket to Chamonix.

The ledge was not very big, even after an hour or so of excavation. I lay uncomfortably in my sleeping bag, with my head propped up by an immovable rock. In order to make the most of the space available, we had ended up making two tiers. John was on the lower shelf of rock and gravel that we had shaped into a makeshift bivouac. He had curled up into the foetal position to stop his long legs hanging over the side. Climbing equipment lay scattered all around. Ropes attached to our harnesses ran out of our sleeping bags and were tied to anchors in the rock above. They needed to be. We were spending our second night on the North Face of the Eiger.

It was strange that such a large mountain face did not overlook other mountains. At the base lay lush green foothills, rather than the usual glaciers and moraine. I could make out the faint sound of cow bells drifting up from alpine meadows over 1,000 metres below. Later, as it got dark, I could see lights flickering from farmhouses. It was an incredible place to spend a night.

We had planned to be higher up the face, but had run into a waterfall just above our ledge in the late afternoon. The feature – known as the Ramp – was renowned for this occurrence. Rather than get a soaking through pressing on, we had reasoned that it was better to stay where we were and hope that an overnight freeze would stem the flow of water.

I felt content. My time in the Alps was going well. In the previous weeks I had managed to complete the Bonatti Pillar on Les Dru with an old school friend, John Taylor, and a new route on the North Face of the Grandes Charmoz with Chris Dale, whom I had met for the first time just a few days before on the campsite. The climbs had been good preparation for the Eiger and had kept me occupied until John's guiding work had finished and he was free to climb with me. Now the night was clear and the weather seemed to be holding. Barring some serious mishap, we would reach the top the following day. It was nice to feel this way after a nervous start.

The day before we left Chamonix, a Welsh climber, Crag Jones, approached John and me on the campsite. He had heard of our trip to the Eiger and wanted to tag along. We both had our reservations about climbing on a rope of three, as it is generally much more complicated and time-consuming. We knew that on the Eiger's huge and complex North Face moving quickly would be crucial to our safety and success, but Crag's powers of persuasion won in the end. Besides, he was a nice guy, easy to get on with, and a good competent climber. Having driven across the Alps from Chamonix to the small town of Grindelwald, following a promising weather forecast, we spent the night in John's camper van. We must have looked like climbers because in the town that night an American tourist stopped me in the street.

'Howdy. D'ya mind telling me which mountain is the Eiger?' the man asked. To me it seemed ridiculous that he could not recognise one of the most famous mountain faces in the world. I laughed openly and dismissively pointed at a mountain towering over the town.

'That was very rude,' John pointed out a little further down the street. 'Besides which, the Eiger is that mountain over there.' He waved at the distinctive outline of another peak further up the valley.

'Sorry,' I replied, feeling very small.

We had caught a train to reach the foot of the mountain. The train, which wound under and inside the Eiger in a tunnel, to reach the summit of the Jungfrau, had been packed with tourists. We were the only climbers. During the course of the journey, people whispered about us, pointed and stared. Finally, someone asked what we knew everyone else was thinking. 'Are you going to climb the Eiger North Face?' When we nodded our replies, a murmur ran down the carriage. Horrified expressions filled people's faces, followed by looks of sorrow. It was obvious we had been written off, already consigned by others on the train to the Eiger's long list of victims.

I had realised before that many people viewed climbing as a crazy activity, whose participants had a reckless disregard for their own safety. Quite simply, most people thought we were mad, but I felt the tourists in the railway carriage were seeing us in a slightly more sinister way. Never before had I felt such an outsider, so misunderstood by most other people. Since what we were about to undertake was so contrary to what they considered normal or acceptable behaviour, it seemed we were no longer human in their eyes. I felt as if we were no longer real people, but merely a spectacle laid on for their enjoyment, a reinforcement of their opinion that the penalty for our deviance from society's norms was likely to be death.

I wondered how racing-car drivers or motorcyclists felt, knowing that many of the spectators came to watch them race expecting to see a few crashes, although most would not admit to the fact. However, car and motorcycle racing are much more mainstream sports than mountaineering, with huge support from sponsors, the media and fans who all have some understanding of what it is like for the participants because they themselves drive or ride. There is no such understanding from some people for mountaineers. On the train up to the Eiger I felt the only role we were expected to play in the tourists' day out was to provide some morbid entertainment.

'Let's get away from this lot,' John had said, as we got off the train at Kleine Scheidegg, where crowds of people were scanning the Eiger's North Face with telescopes and binoculars. 'They make me sick.'

We neither wanted nor needed recognition from others. The climb was simply a shared personal ambition and to receive such attention was a very unsettling way to start a long and serious climb. However, as with the starting-off points to many climbs in the Alps, the tourists soon fell away. They did not stray far from the world of railways, cable cars, stations, shops and restaurants that they were familiar and comfortable with. We walked a few hundred metres away from the station towards the face and soon found ourselves alone, surrounded by flowers in a beautiful alpine meadow. The Eiger's daunting North Face towered above, looking strangely out of place. I struggled to tip my head back far enough to see the summit and to comprehend the enormity of the sight.

The base of the mountain arrived quickly. It took little more than an hour from the railway station to walk to a point where the grass reached scree dotted with small rock buttresses. The slope reared up and gradually increased in angle, until it ran into patches of snow and ice much higher up on the face proper.

At around midday we started zig-zagging up faint and indistinct paths, which at least gave some idea we were heading in the right direction. However, I had been fooled by such paths in the past; they sometimes ended abruptly below a blank wall or similarly unclimbable feature and seemed to emphasise that you should follow your own judgments and not those of others who had been before. Vast quantities of loose rock which had fallen from above lay everywhere. Moving without dislodging any was difficult and we had to be very careful to avoid knocking it down on each other.

'I think it's time to rope up,' John announced when we arrived below the first rock wall.

The terrain was steepening. Above were huge limestone walls that formed the right-hand side of the face and to our left was a pillar that I knew led up to below the First Icefield on our route. The level at which we traversed left was crucial to reaching the icefield.

John tied on to the ends of both ropes, while Crag and I tied on to one each. Then John led off. We followed simultaneously, just a few metres apart. Almost immediately, Crag's rope hooked around a loose rock on a ledge, flipping it off. It bounced down towards me.

'Careful,' I shouted, stepping sideways out of the rock's path. Crag raised his hands by way of apology and we scrambled on. We regularly dislodged rocks which crashed down, before eventually coming to rest on ledges further down. By moving sideways, one way then the other, I managed to keep out of the line of fire.

'Oh, look at these ropes,' John sighed, as I reached the ledge where he was belayed. As both Crag and I had moved around each other the ropes had crossed many times and had become tangled. John pulled at the pile of rope spaghetti between himself, Crag and me, getting more and more frustrated as the lines stubbornly refused to separate. 'You're going to have to untie, Simon,' he said finally.

With one rope free John quickly sorted the tangle, but time was drifting by. It was already mid-afternoon and we had not even reached the first difficult section of the climb. Worrying clouds were beginning to swirl around the top of the face. I led the next pitch and once again it was necessary to free a tangle from the ropes. Dealing with the ropes became a time-consuming struggle and by the time we reached the Difficult Crack it was late afternoon. We gathered on a broad shelf below the steep, ice-lined corner. The ground above looked significantly harder than anything we had already encountered. The atmosphere between the three of us felt tense.

'I'm sorry guys,' Crag said in soft Welsh tones. 'I think it's best if I go down.' Neither John or I were going to disagree. Climbing as a three had not worked out as we had naïvely hoped it would. We all knew as much. As last to join, Crag was doing the honourable thing by offering to leave.

We sorted through our rucksacks and exchanged some gear. Crag gave me some food and a set of billies, which we would need to cook on. I handed him a spare rope and some slings that would enable him to make the few abseils down to where he would be able to scramble off.

'Good luck,' he said generously, once he was ready to go. Then he clipped his rope to our belay and abseiled away from me. Once the abseil was completed, I waved and tossed the rope into the void below, before turning my attention back to John climbing above, who was struggling to scrape ice out of a crack in the steep corner. The Difficult Crack certainly seemed to be living up to its name.

I watched John carefully as he chopped ice away from the rock above him, before pulling up strenuously and bridging his feet out on the walls of the corner so that he could stand in balance to clear the next section of ice. Fortunately, the difficulty did not last long. After a few moves John was able to grab the rope hanging down the corner and use that to aid his progress above. I soon found myself following the pitch.

'Look, there's a rope across the traverse,' John said when I reached him.

A rope led horizontally to the left across a steep slab. This was the famous Hinterstoisser Traverse, the scene of many epics and tragedies in the past. For many years the traverse was considered irreversible and was the scene of an infamous tragic accident after the Austrian Toni Kurtz was unable to retreat across it during an early attempt on the Face and died trying to reach the safety of the nearby railway viewing gallery. It was strange to be looking up at the gallery, knowing that a railway ran up through a tunnel inside the mountain. The window allowed tourists to view the Face on their way up to the summit of the Jungfraujoch. Climbers had used the window to access the railway and made escapes down along its tracks. In some ways it was a shame the rope was in place as I would have liked to have traversed the slab for myself, but having wasted so much time already, there was also an element of relief. Barely pausing to take the equipment from John, I swung across the ropes and quickly reached a shelf that led leftwards to the First Icefield. Half way along was a small cave banked up with snow at its back, but which I knew would dig out to provide a sufficient shelter for the night. This was known as the Swallow's Nest, another feature etched into mountaineering folklore.

'Come across, John,' I screamed. 'I've found an ace doss for the night.'

Now, a day after our first few hours on the face I flinched, recalling our initial encounter with the mountain. I felt much more comfortable with my surroundings and knew that both John and I were climbing well as a team. Yet still the sense of occasion played on my mind. The North Face of the Eiger is simply one of the most famous and notorious mountain climbs in the world. First climbed in 1938 after a series of high profile and sometimes fatal attempts, it has continued to lure climbers from all over the world. Over the years many dramas, epics and controversies had been played out on the huge wall.

Our second day passed much more smoothly until we were stopped by the waterfall pouring down the Ramp. The previous afternoon's threatening cloud cleared in the night and we had awoken to a clear day. The features etched into my mind from reading books and articles passed in quick succession: the First and Second Icefields were connected by the Ice Hose – a steep couloir lined with water-ice. We had moved quickly up the icefields themselves, climbing together until the leader had placed all of our ice-screws, when the second would bring them up and take over in front. And all the time the Face, which had a terrible reputation for rockfall, stayed silent. We had timed our attempt well and the loose rock higher on the Face was held firmly in place by snow and ice from the recent storm. However, that meant that the steep cracks which led from the Second Icefield to the Flatiron were awkwardly choked with ice. We had passed the site of Death

Bivouac too early in the day to consider spending the night there ourselves, choosing instead to cross the Third Icefield. There a single stone had fallen from above and ricocheted from the ice a few metres to my side in the most notable event of an otherwise incident-free day.

It had been amazing to view these places, which for so long had been just names in books. I sensed the history all around. Old woollen balaclavas, gloves, pieces of bleached rope, cord, pitons, ice-screws, karabiners, tents half-frozen into the ice and a host of other items lay abandoned on the mountain. As we passed these pieces of ancient gear I wondered about the stories behind them. Whether their owners were going up or down, if they were successful or not, and occasionally if pieces of gear in unlikely locations marked the site of a tragedy or accident. It made the entire climb feel very special and unique, as if it was a living climbing museum.

On our third day on the Face we woke to near-silence. The cold of the night had done what we hoped for. The waterfall further up the Ramp was no longer running. After a quick brew and a bite to eat, we headed off. I climbed swiftly up easy ground to the base of the waterfall and belayed. A little water was still dripping down, but much had frozen over rocks in a steep corner. The rock was clearly visible through the ice, indicating the ice was rarely more than a few millimetres thick. I felt relieved that I was not going to have to lead the next pitch. It was obviously going to be very difficult.

As I settled down to belay, I remembered the party above us who had climbed the waterfall the previous afternoon. They had obviously got very wet and I wondered how their night had been. Initially I was pleased that we had settled for our drier option. Then, as John began climbing with a scurry of grating ice-axes and slipping crampons, I wondered if climbing through the waterfall was not so bad after all.

John's progress was desperately slow and precarious. Sometimes he would use his axes placed in very thin ice, and at others simply hooked over small ledges in the rock. Often he would chop the ice away, drop his axes to hang from their wrist loops and then use the manufactured handholds instead. It was ugly, inelegant climbing to watch as he tried out many different holds and axe placements before committing himself and moving upwards. Each move was accompanied by skating crampons. There were several occasions when he seemed to be falling, with both feet flying off simultaneously, or an axe placement pulling out. Sometimes one side of his body lost contact and swung out like a door before he restored control. Every time the situation looked desperate I took a deep breath and braced myself, ready to hold a fall.

The fall never came. Somehow John clawed his way up the pitch and shouted down for me to follow. The climbing did not seem so bad coming second, but I still struggled. In some places holds had been cleared of ice and in others axe placements formed, making figuring out the moves that much easier. However, on other occasions much of the ice needed to make the next moves had been hacked and kicked away. At such moments I was grateful for the comfort which the tight rope from above provided. The difficulties were steep and fierce, but quite short. Soon I pulled up out of the corner and on to a small patch of ice. It had been this ice melting in the heat of the afternoon that had caused the waterfall. John was belayed at the top.

'Good lead,' I said when I reached him, impressed that he had successfully climbed such a difficult pitch cold, first thing in the morning.

'I think we go right, soon.'

'I hope so,' I replied, well aware that since beginning the climb we had been moving leftwards across the huge face. The climb finished above a small icefield called the Spider, back in the centre of the face. Groups often got into difficulties misjudging when to traverse rightwards to reach it.

I took some gear from John and moved out to a rock rib on the right. The climbing above was very exposed. Below me a climber I knew – Dai Lampard – was crossing the Third Icefield to reach the Ramp. He and his partner Bob Wightman had been following us the day before and for some time we had been close enough to exchange shouted insults. They looked tiny, lost in the vastness of the face, but I could clearly see the concentration on his face as he swung his axes and boots. Fortunately on such a steep piece of rock the handholds were large. I climbed quickly, savouring the position until I pulled up on to a ledge about a metre wide.

'I've found the traverse,' I shouted down triumphantly.

The snow on the ledge had been levelled, where the party in front of us had spent the night. A horizontal shelf of varying width continued rightwards for several hundred metres back into the centre of the face. John's face broke into a broad smile when he joined me. I could hear him shrieking with delight as he shuffled along the ledge. I quickly followed, marvelling at the thought of the climbers making the first ascent, who had no idea that the feature was even there. They would have been very happy to find it. The ledge led straight across to the bottom of the Spider. I could hardly believe that climbing so easy could be possible in such surroundings. Much of the ground above and below was near-vertical, but for most of the length of the ledge it was possible to walk. Just before the Spider the rock below the ledge was actually undercut. The view down to the lower icefields and the meadows at the base of the mountain made me feel dizzy.

'We're going to make it,' John said excitedly. 'We'll get off the mountain today.'

I had not entertained such thoughts before, as I thought much difficult climbing would still lie above us, but the easy traverse had changed all that. As we slowly moved into the Spider I knew the top was close and the icefield itself was easy to climb. The ice lay in a small basin with steep walls above. Ancient ropes soared upwards out of the ice in a number of places, fastened to pieces of old ironmongery in the rock above. Only one of them marked the Exit Cracks which led to the summit snow slopes. I began to feel anxious. It was an oppressive place and the abandoned gear showed that it had obviously caused others a lot of distress in the past.

I tentatively looked at a line out of the top left of the

basin, but it was too steep and I gave up after a feeble attempt.

'I'm going to try over there,' I said to John pointing out left. It was not obvious, but the remnants of a rope led horizontally left into a smooth scooped corner.

The traverse was easy, but once I reached the corner, the climbing became difficult. The rock had changed from the more accommodating limestone below to a compact shale. I was climbing up what appeared to be a water-worn runnel about two metres wide. The bedding in the rock pointed down towards me, so there were no real handholds to speak of. I moved delicately upwards by bridging across the runnel with my arms and legs, transferring weight from one side of my body to the other. After maybe ten or fifteen metres I knew that I simply must not fall off. There was a large ledge below. If I fell I would hit it and be badly injured. A retreat down the face was now inconceivable, and a lone climber would find it very demanding to climb the ground I was now negotiating, in order to go and get assistance. I simply could not mess up.

As I got higher, the potential length of a fall increased. The angle did begin to ease, but at the same time the runnel broadened, making it increasingly difficult to bridge. I balanced upwards towards the summit slopes that were now clearly visible. Then suddenly I noticed an old metal peg sticking from the rock about ten metres above me. It offered a lifeline. If I could reach the peg I would be secure. By opposing pressures between hands and feet and different sides of the body I somehow maintained upward movement, but it almost felt like an out-of-body experience. As I approached the peg, my position was getting desperate, my legs unbearably tired. I lunged for the peg, grabbed it and pulled myself up level with it. The peg fell in my hand. For a moment I thought I was off, but somehow I steadied myself. I stood in balance and nervously tapped the peg back into the rock with my ice-hammer and clipped a rope to it.

The climbing above eased and I was soon established on the summit slopes. Triumphantly I wound an ice-screw into the summit icefield, clipped into it and slumped against the ice. Having broken out of the confines of the basin below, a panorama had opened out again. Several pitches were required to climb the icefield. Higher up the angle eased to an annoying point where it was barely steep enough to climb, but still too steep to walk up. Whenever I watched John climbing this section, it looked as if he was crawling. Finally, John ran out the rope to reach the summit ridge. A set of deep steps in the snow made by other climbers coming up the Mitelleggi Ridge led up to the top.

Now there was lots of space and big drops on both sides. The line of steps followed the exact crest of the ridge. Maybe it was this space, the steps in the ridge or perhaps the contrast with the steep confined climbing below, but whatever the reason, I began to feel dizzy. After a few minutes I realised I was having an attack of vertigo. My sense of balance temporarily deserted me and I had to concentrate very hard simply to place my feet in the bucket-sized steps that ran along the gently angled ridge. I struggled to lead a rope length, take a belay on the ridge and bring John up to me. He continued to the summit and once he was established on the top I crawled up to join him.

Eventually there was no further to climb. John shook my hand when I arrived and then giggled hysterically as we balanced together on the tiny pyramid of snow that formed the top. Then I sat shoulder to shoulder with him, feeling nauseous but admiring the view.

Later, as we walked off down the West Flank of the mountain, the nausea was replaced by a feeling of fulfilment and calm. It had been a good year for climbing. There had been the ascent in Peru, the Bonatti Pillar, the new route on Les Grandes Charmoz and now the Eiger.

Near the foot of the mountain, we caught up with the party which had been in front of us. It turned out they were Germans. We shook hands, congratulated each other and arranged to meet in the hotel below for a celebratory beer.

They seemed an unlikely pairing when they came into the

bar some time later. I had not really noticed on the mountain, but it was uncommon to see a teenage boy climbing with a much older man, especially on such a demanding route.

'He is my father,' the boy explained, as the older man went to the bar.

'Amazing,' I said. 'And how old are you?'

'Sixteen.'

'And your father?'

'Sixty.'

John shrieked with laughter, which under the circumstances I knew to be a sign of deep respect. We congratulated the older man again when he came back with the drinks.

'I was too tired today,' he said modestly. 'My son had to lead all the way.'

We talked for some time and shared some experiences. Through broken English they related a remarkable story. The father had been on the Eiger forty years before, but had been hit by a stone that had injured his arm and forced a retreat. His desire to climb the route had remained, but he had not returned until now. Earlier that summer the man had lost his wife and the boy his mother. Rather than sink into the depression and apathy you would have expected, they had decided they would spend their summer climbing. They had set themselves a series of challenges, with the North Face of the Eiger as their ultimate goal.

The Germans said their goodbyes and left for Grindelwald. John and I made ourselves comfortable in the bar at Kleine Scheidegg, and by the time we staggered outside the last train had already left. Neither of us fancied walking down the railway tracks to the town that evening and reasoned that, having spent two nights out on the face, we deserved a night with a roof over our heads. We started casting around for likely places. After a short search we found a door open round the back of the hotel. In our drunken, happy state we saw little harm in spending a night in the laundry room and quickly made ourselves comfortable.

Although I was very tired I found it difficult to sleep. My

body was still full of adrenalin and my mind racing. I thought about the climb and relived some of the crucial moments, but it was mostly the German father and son that occupied my mind. I admired them and I felt we had something in common.

In the previous months we had all been involved in personal tragedy. The Germans had suffered a close bereavement and I had experienced a particularly harrowing mountaineering accident, where Joe had come close to dying. What we shared was our response to those events. Perhaps living with the threat of death while climbing had made us all more able to accommodate death. Neither the Germans nor I had allowed the negatives of bad experiences to override what we considered to be very positive in our lives. Rather than back away from life and retreat into ourselves fearing death, we had decided to carry on as before. In the case of the German man, his wife's death had probably reminded him of his own increasing age and spurred him on to fulfil his climbing ambitions while he was still capable.

In the morning I lay in my sleeping bag now aware of the aches and exaggerated tiredness that comes after climbing such a route. The gas stove between John and me was purring, heating water for a brew. Damp clothing lay scattered over the floor from the previous evening. It appeared to be drying nicely. Then the laundry door swung open. A woman walked in and viewed the scene before starting to scream. Then she hurried away and returned a few minutes later with the manager.

'Last night you were in my bar. If you wanted a room you should have said,' he shouted. 'You must pay!'

John and I smiled at each other. We had hoped to slip away before anyone discovered us. We knew we would be unable to pay. The manager looked even more angry.

'I will bring my book,' he explained with the usual Swiss efficiency, before strutting out of the room.

'What shall we do?' I asked.

'Let's leg it,' John replied, already out of his sleeping bag.

In a frenzy of packing we stuffed our rucksacks, put on our boots and slipped out of the door. Then we ran off down the railway tracks giggling.

'Some people just don't understand,' I said as we paused to get our breath.

'Understand what?'

'People like us.'

Chapter Three

Going East

I lay on the pile of bags and closed my eyes trying to relax. It was difficult as my other senses started working overtime. The warm, damp air seemed saturated with smells: a heady cocktail of raw sewage, urine, spices and wood smoke. Other smells drifted in and out of the mix, some familiar, some strangely exotic. It was reasonably quiet, but occasionally a motorised rickshaw passed. Each vehicle produced a distinctive high-pitched whine, which increased to an annoying level before fading into the distance.

A winter at home had passed since the Eiger climb. While the weather remained good I had occupied myself climbing most days with groups of friends on the gritstone outcrops of the Peak District. Dank November and December days stopped most outdoor activity, but my time passed pleasantly enough, working out in gymnasiums and indoor climbing walls, or simply socialising in one of the many households that formed the extended community of climbers on the west side of Sheffield. A couple of months of superb winter climbing and guiding in Scotland had taken me through to spring and provided just enough money for a trip away. I had found myself in Pakistan after a geologist called Mike Searle had invited a group of his colleagues and a contingent of climbers to join him exploring the valleys above a village called Hushe in the Pakistani Karakoram.

I must have dozed off because I woke to a lot more noise. Opening my eyes was a shock. It was now light and we were surrounded by hundreds of men dressed in the baggy light cotton trousers and long shirts that are known in Pakistan as Shalwar Kameez. I looked around anxiously. It was reassuring to see my friend Craig Kentwell sitting on the other side of the pile of luggage. For a moment I thought he had left me. To save money we had taken flights from Britain to the city of Karachi in the south of the country. Now we sat at the entrance to Karachi Railway Station, hoping to start the long journey to the mountains, which lay nearly two thousand kilometres to the north. What had been a quiet spot when we had arrived in the night was now a bustling market. Traders were erecting stalls all around and passengers were arriving to catch trains. With our white faces and huge pile of luggage we were very conspicuous. The men simply stood and stared. Craig put on a pair of sunglasses and stared straight back at them.

'What is so interesting?' I asked.

'Us.'

'How long have this lot been here?'

'Since it got light, about half an hour ago.'

It was intimidating and I felt vulnerable, imagining that the crowd could rush forward and overpower us at any moment. However, I quickly realised that nobody had that intention.

'I guess we're providing today's entertainment,' Craig said.

'Where are the others?'

'They're having some breakfast over there.' Craig pointed down the road to a row of restaurants. 'We're leaving in about an hour.'

Craig, a laid-back Australian on a prolonged world tour, seemed to be taking it all in his stride. But I found the piercing stares from the ever-increasing crowd uncomfortable, if no longer threatening.

The sun was now above the buildings. It was stiflingly hot and I already felt as if I was starting to melt. I unzipped a kit bag to get out my water bottle and the crowd jostled for position, trying to get a clearer view of what I was doing. I pulled the bottle out, showed it around, unscrewed the top and drank from it. Everyone looked at me as if I had just performed some sort of miracle.

'Now I know what an animal in a zoo feels like,' I said to Craig. I could tell it was going to be a long, hot and demanding day.

Twenty-six hours later we climbed down from a railway carriage in Rawalpindi. It had been an epic journey. Our travels had taken us up through Sind and the Punjab in early summer. To say it had been hot would be a gross understatement. In the middle of the day in the Sind Desert it had been 46 degrees Celsius. There was no escaping such heat, which is well above body temperature. Even with the fans inside the carriage and open windows, the air rushing by felt like the hot blast you get opening an oven door. However, moving air did at least wick away sweat and enable our bodies to cool themselves. Whenever the train stopped, which it did with annoying regularity, sweat simply poured from our skin. At each station we staggered out to rehydrate, frantically downing bottled drinks before the train pulled off again.

To add further discomfort, we had been unable to obtain seats at such short notice. We sat on the floor for the entire journey, squeezed into a small space at the end of a carriage next to the toilets. While the train moved, people were continually walking over us to get to the lavatory or passing through into the next carriage. Whenever it stopped they trampled over us in a manic rush to get on and off. The toilet, which was simply a hole in the floor directly on to the track, stank all the way.

But despite the discomfort, I began to enjoy the place. People behaved so differently from my normal experience that everything seemed peculiar. There was obviously some level of social order operating, but it was difficult to understand. People appeared less encumbered with rules than I was used to and that gave the place a romantic charm. I could feel an undefinable freedom, that I sensed had been lost at home.

I had found my time in Peru eye-opening, but here there seemed so much to observe and absorb. The sights, sounds and smells of this strange and alien place were almost overwhelming. But I found the feeling of being just about able to cope exhilarating. I knew I simply had to adapt to the changed circumstances and operate within them confidently.

By climbing standards our trip was not particularly successful. We had arrived very early in the season and found the mountains still in the grip of winter. Later, after the snow had cleared, we had been plagued by bad weather. However, we had managed to bag a few minor peaks.

Our lack of success in the mountains hardly seemed to matter. What stuck in my mind was the landscape. Snow-capped mountains towered above deep valleys cut into stone and rubble, forming a land of bare earth, dust and rock. Huge, muddy-brown rivers roared along the bottom of the valleys. Close up, their sound was deafening. The ground shook from rocks being rolled along the riverbed by the force of the flowing water.

It was a place where changes in the landscape that are usually imperceptibly slow were instant and visible. The mountains were growing and the rivers were cutting down into them. Landslides crashed down and blocked roads, rivers changed course and washed villages away and pulses of mud poured down hillsides burying all in their track. The powers at work were scary, but exhilarating. These were raw and rugged mountains, without any of the chocolate-box charm of the Alps. To me that made them all the more interesting. The beauty of the place was the mountains themselves, rather than their place in a wider composition, as a backdrop to flowery meadows, pine trees and log cabins.

If the landscape was impressive, what was most surprising was that people actually lived among it all. To me it seemed a truly ridiculous place to inhabit – a place that would only provide trouble and strife. In many ways this was true. Those who lived in the Karakoram had not tamed the place, but learned to manage the land to give them a marginal existence. In among the brown, desolate panoramas were splashes of radiant green. These areas of cultivated land always ran down hillsides below the water channels that irrigated them. Their size varied from just a handful of tiny fields to entire irrigated valleys, with numerous villages and towns.

Once our trip was over and I was back at home, images of Pakistan often flashed through my mind. Momentarily I would find myself on a bus following the Karakoram Highway with the Indus River roaring far below, or riding a jeep through showers of apricot blossom, or walking along irrigation ditches among a patchwork of tiny green fields – or high on a mountain looking down on highways of glacial ice far below.

We sat at the edge of a huge glacier amongst boulders scattered on the ice. I looked around. Some of the rocks were as big as cars and precariously balanced on pillars of creaking ice. Occasionally there was a loud crash as one of the rocks slipped off its pedestal. At the edge of the glacial ice-falls, cliffs and snow slopes marked the base of the peaks that jutted up steeply all around. It was a truly dramatic and elemental place. Up here there was nothing but ice, rock and the little streams of melt water that ran down the glacier in the heat of the day.

The mountain we had come to attempt towered above us. It had entered my thoughts regularly since I had first set eyes on it the year before. At 6,300 metres in height, Leyla Peak was no giant by Himalayan standards, but it was one of the most beautiful mountains I had ever seen. The bulging granite walls at its base guarded a symmetrical icy pyramid above. It looked like a sculpture. Ever since I had first glimpsed it through a gap in the clouds, I imagined somehow breaking through the granite walls to climb the perfect snowy ridge which lay above. That moment, along with many others on my first visit to Pakistan the previous year, had made a lasting impression which had compelled me to return.

'It's your bid Simon,' Tom Curtis said, nudging me in the ribs.

'Sorry, three clubs,' I replied, somewhat startled, wondering how long I had been daydreaming.

It seemed a little strange to be playing bridge before starting what was likely to be a long and serious climb, but the game had become compelling. Perhaps it was because it occupied all four of us, or simply that it fitted into our relaxed approach. Having spent the previous night sleeping under a large boulder about three hours' walk down the valley, our initial plan had been to start climbing as soon as we arrived at the foot of the mountain. Then on arrival we changed our minds. Breaching the steep granite was going to be the difficult, time-consuming part of the climb and therefore it was best to spend the night below it and get an early start the next day. However, we reckoned we could reach the bottom of the wall in two or three hours from the glacier. Faced with the choice of spending most of the day on a cramped bivouac ledge, or lounging around where we were until late afternoon, we chose the latter. Tom had suggested a game of cards.

The year before a mutual friend had recommended that Tom Curtis and I should climb together, when I was looking for a climbing partner after returning from Pakistan. Two weeks of drinking in rain-soaked Chamonix, followed by two days of fearfully hard climbing had cemented our friendship. My enthusiasm for some of the mountains that I had seen while I had been away must have been contagious, because we had agreed to organise a trip to Pakistan together for the following year. Tom returned to Brazil to continue his research work with ponds of sewage and we made our plans through infrequent letters. He had returned to Britain only a few days before the trip. In a frantic evening we had tried to make the final arrangements, but it had been difficult in the noisy, alcoholic setting of a busy house party. A few of us left for Pakistan early and then Tom caught us up in the north of the country at a hotel in the town of Gilgit.

'I've lost the gas,' he had announced on arrival.

'How come?'

'When they checked my hand luggage in the airport they found it and took it off me. Said it was unsafe.'

'But,' I shouted, 'why did you not put the cylinders in your check-in luggage like I told you?'

Tom held up his hands in apology. 'Sorry, I guess I'll have to do the honourable thing.'

'What?' I demanded.

'Impale myself on my ice-axe.'

Tom made me laugh at myself. He had the ability to turn any situation into farce, making light of even the most serious problems. His enthusiasm quickly banished other negative thoughts, and when we searched the local bazaars we soon managed to find some replacement gas cylinders.

The day passed pleasantly. Occasionally someone would put on a stove and make a hot drink and at lunchtime we each ate a bowl of instant noodles. However, the game of bridge held most of our attention. At times I almost forgot about the mountains all around.

'What do you think?' I asked Sean at two o'clock.

'Give it another hour,' he replied casually, barely looking up from his cards. The hour soon passed.

'Let's give it half an hour more,' Tom said.

I could see Andy Cave, the youngest of our team, raising his eyebrows. We had found him at a loose end, walking the streets of Gilgit, having already climbed a mountain called Tupodam with another group of friends, who had since left for home. He had about a month of free time before he travelled to Nepal to attempt another peak.

'I think we'd better go,' Andy said finally, his patience stretched to the limit.

We put the cards away, packed up, shouldered our rucksacks and set off across the glacier. To begin with it was very easy walking over bare ice, but as we got higher, there was snow lying on top. Once there was a good covering we stopped and roped together, to prevent anyone falling into a crevasse blanketed in snow.

We made steady progress into a small basin with a lake in the bottom. At the back of the lake easy granite slabs led up to a glacier. The front of the glacier formed a wall of ice up to a hundred metres high and several hundred across, which hung above the slabs. At the right edge of the glacier a gully led up between the wall of ice and steeper rock slabs. The gully offered the easiest route on to an easy-angled snow slope above. It was obvious from the blocks of ice scattered below and floating in the lake that chunks fell off the ice-cliff from time to time.

When we reached the rock, I paused.

'I say we take the ropes off and leg it.'

There were no objections. The less time we spent below the ice-cliff the less likely we were to suffer ice falling from it. We untied the ropes, packed them away and then immediately began zig-zagging up the slabs.

I could feel the tension. It was as if we were trying to hide from someone, as if the ice hanging above was a living enemy which would open fire if we were detected. We all moved silently, carefully tip-toeing around loose boulders that lay on the slab, well aware that any clumsy slip had the potential to send rocks crashing down, which might in turn trigger a section of ice to collapse. But mostly our survival lay in fate. If a large section of cliff fell above us, we would be killed. Yet despite the danger I felt a strange and sickening excitement in what we were doing.

The previous week of heavy exertion had served us well. Although with food, gas, equipment and spare clothing we all had in excess of 25 kilos on our backs, we were moving quickly. In half an hour of intense climbing we reached the base of the gully that led up to the snow slope where we hoped to spend the night. Now it was possible to look across to the left to the base of the ice-cliff. I knew the danger had passed and began to relax, the tension and fear replaced by a feeling of awe.

We had gained height rapidly climbing the slabs and now it was possible to appreciate our position. I looked at the lake below, the glacial highways stretching to the north and west, the shadows of mountains lengthening across the valley below and the nearby peaks beginning to turn yellow in the evening sun.

Soon I returned to the climbing, aware that we still had to go higher before finding a spot to settle down for the night. The rock ran into snow and I paused to fit crampons to my boots and to take an ice-axe from my rucksack. As the gully narrowed towards its top, the slope became steeper. A thin sheet of ice ran over the rock below. It gave awkward, insecure climbing. I balanced up the ice using my free hand to steady myself to make new axe placements, which were never deep enough to hold a fall should I slip. I knew I was struggling when Andy stopped following me and simply stood and watched. After ten metres of climbing that was beginning to stretch me, I came out of the top of the narrowing gully and some rock reappeared. I stepped left on to the slab and found a welcome ledge. The danger had passed.

'Do you want a rope on that?' I shouted down.

'I like beer and shagging,' Andy replied. 'Drop me a rope.'

I laughed. Andy possessed wisdom beyond his age and was not going to take unnecessary risks. At sixteen he had followed his father into a Yorkshire coal mine. When the miners went on strike in 1984, rather than stand on a picket line, Andy spent his days climbing. I often met him at crags around the Peak District. His appetite for the sport seemed insatiable and his standard soared. When the strike finally ended he lasted just two days back at his old job, before handing in his notice. He was no longer satisfied by the daily routine and the claustrophobic surroundings of work in the mines. Andy moved into Sheffield to be closer to the Peak District and signed on for a while before going to college. For him, the freedom and adventure he found through climbing were more important than a steady job and a regular wage. He happily traded in security for a life that was much more uncertain, but infinitely more enjoyable and exciting.

I pulled the rope from my rucksack, uncoiled it, tied on and dropped the other end down to Andy. Then, as he began to climb, I flipped a nylon sling over a flake of rock and clipped myself to it. Andy stylishly moved through the section of climbing that I had grovelled my way up.

'Cheers mate,' he said as he reached me, discarding his end of the rope. I lowered the rope back down for Sean, while Andy moved steadily up the slope above.

We were now in a higher basin, formed by a glacier whose front edge dropped away in the ice-cliffs we had just skirted round. Above, snow slopes led up to the steep granite wall we would need to breach in order to get established on the upper part of the mountain. On the right-hand side of the basin I could make out a thin ribbon of ice running down the rock and on to the snow. The ice broadened higher up and filled the back of a deep gully. It was this feature we hoped to climb, as it cut right through the band of steep rock, but it had been difficult to tell from below if this would be possible. Closer up, our prospects looked more promising.

Once everyone was safely up the difficult section I recoiled the rope and followed them up the slope.

'I guess we'll spend the night here,' said Sean, when we reached the ice. By cutting into the nearby soft snow where it was lying up against the rock, we were quickly able to produce a platform that was almost wide enough to lie down on. But before we could get into our sleeping bags we all took turns to walk down the slope about ten metres below the camp, tied to a length of rope. Then we dug a hole, went to the toilet and filled it in again, before returning to the platform. The hygiene and sanitation standards in the towns and villages we had travelled through on our way to the mountains had been poor. In the nearest village – Hushe – a water-filled channel ran down the main street. People drew water and washed pots, clothes and their bodies in the same channel. We had all suffered stomach problems and learned to live with the constant threat of diarrhoea. Perhaps it was his work with sewage that had given Tom some immunity, but he was the only one not directly affected.

'God, you all stink,' he said, as we finished the toilet ritual. Although he was not ill, it seemed he was suffering nearly as much as the rest of us.

We settled down to melting snow for drinks and preparing some food.

'Who's for Imodium?' I asked as we finished our meals.

'Why not,' Andy and Sean chorused, taking a capsule each from the bottle I handed them. Then I took one myself, silently hoping it would work effectively. I did not want to spend the night getting up to go to the toilet.

In the morning we woke to another good day and readied ourselves. I had been able to enjoy the warmth of my sleeping bag without interruptions and the bivouac was so luxurious that I could operate the stove without getting up. After a brew and a bowl of porridge it was time to leave.

I unzipped my waterproof bivouac bag and the sleeping bag inside and stood up. The Imodium the night before had stemmed the flow of liquid through my bowels, but not the wind. An awful smell filled the air.

'That's disgusting,' Tom just had time to say, before throwing up his breakfast into the snow.

'Sorry,' I said feebly.

Tom's retching continued for most of the time it took to pack. It was not a good start to his day. Then Tom and Andy moved away from the platform and set up a belay at the base of the ice-ribbon. Andy made short work of the steep section and disappeared from sight into the gully above. Tom paid out rope quickly and by the time Sean and I joined him, Andy was shouting down that he was safe. He pulled up the slack rope and Tom started climbing.

It was still early and we were not yet in the sunlight, but the upper section of the face was bathed in light and was already warm. I could hear water running down the rock at the back of the ice. Suddenly, there was a dull thud from above. I looked up to see Tom removing his ice-axe from a large hole, before searching around for another placement. The axe had chopped straight through the ice, exposing bare rock below.

'Bit thin here,' he shouted down, before chopping away some more ice.

'Hey, save some for us,' Sean shouted up.

Tom scratched his way up the section of thin ice, and it took a good lead by Sean to get us both established, in the gully above. A rope-length of easy climbing ran up to a serious steepening of the gully into a corner. The left wall was coated in ice and it was this that Andy was already climbing.

Sean climbed up to join me and led off up the ice. At the top of the pitch he set up a belay. Soon I was following. The ice, although near-vertical, was perfect and accepted each blow of the axe first time. It felt very secure and now the sun had reached us, I began to enjoy the climbing. I only paused briefly at the belay while Sean handed me some gear, and then carried on upwards. The others were moving nicely above.

Then, about twenty metres above, I started to feel cramps in my stomach. At first they were only mild and I continued climbing, but after just a few more moves they became unbearable. I stopped, realising I needed to act quickly. In a hasty manoeuvre I put a nylon sling under my arms and clipped it to the ice-screw. Then I tied the rope to the screw, before removing my harness. All that was now holding me was the sling tight under each armpit. If I slipped out of it I would be gone. I pulled my trousers down with little time to spare and emptied myself down the ice below, while Sean looked up in horror.

Putting the clothing and harness back on again caused more problems, but at least I could take my time. When Sean came to follow he climbed well to one side of the stain down the ice.

'That looked a bit desperate,' he said at the belay. 'I'm glad you weren't directly above me.'

'Yeah,' I replied. 'That would have presented me with

a dilemma, you or my salopettes. It would have been a tough call.'

My stomach seemed to quieten down and we climbed slowly, enjoying the perfect ice. After six rope-lengths the angle eased. The climbing was still absorbing, following runnels of ice up rock slabs, but I knew we had completed the most difficult section. By late afternoon we had reached a place just below the snow ridge, which led uninterrupted to the summit. The weather was closing in and there were no obvious places to spend the night on the ridge. I dug a little and found the snow to be quite deep.

'Let's spend the night here,' I said, beginning to enlarge one of the pits in the snow. Within an hour we dug two snow-holes into the slope. Tom and Andy occupied one while Sean and I took the other.

Inside was cosy and quiet, with the snow all around muffling sounds from outside. It felt very secure. We prepared some drinks and food in comfort. Then, as we began to settle down for the night, I felt a sharp pain in my stomach.

'You couldn't do me a favour, could you Sean?'

'Sure,' he said smiling. I got out of my sleeping bag and reversed out of the entrance tunnel. The smile disappeared from Sean's face.

'Just hold my arms, to stop me falling backwards while I go to the loo, would you?'

In the morning we joined the ridge. Although the technical climbing difficulties were behind us we still gained height slowly, labouring under heavy rucksacks and the effects of the rarefied air. At first the snow was reasonably compact, but as the day wore on it became deeper making each step more of an effort.

The ridge was ruler-straight, with just a small notch at two-thirds height, where it was broken by a thin band of rock. I could not help but stare at where the two wedges of snow on either side of the ridge ended in a nipple of rock set in the dark blue sky. A dainty plume of snow blew from the summit. It was hard to concentrate and climb quickly in the midst of such beauty. I often found myself daydreaming when I was out in front.

Later, a cold wind began to blow and it clouded over. The weather seemed to be taking on a pattern. When the snow came, we all felt confident it would clear later. Sean reached a stance just below the notch.

'See if you can find a place to spend the night over by those rocks,' he said as I joined him.

Now the snow was very deep and I struggled to plough a trench, even though I was moving almost horizontally. The rocks looked less likely to provide a bivouac site the closer I got to them. Then I noticed a small overhang with a shelf perhaps a metre below. As I grew closer it became clear that we would be able dig some sort of platform which would offer some shelter from the elements. I smashed a peg into the rock, tied myself to it and brought Sean across.

'What do you think?' I asked.

'It'll have to do.'

Sean was right. After digging with our axes for a short time we could make the platform no bigger. It was small and would be uncomfortable, but looked by far the best option.

'Room for two more?' Andy asked as he arrived.

'Sorry,' Sean said, shrugging his shoulders. He pointed at the small shelf we had managed to dig and Andy waded back the way he had come.

It was now snowing heavily and we wasted no time getting ready for the night. Once we were inside our sleeping bags we could relax. Melting snow for drinks was time-consuming and occasionally the stove blew out, but the small overhang above us was providing a surprising amount of shelter. Very little snow or wind was reaching us.

Andy and Tom finally settled for a spot at the edge of the rocks about ten metres away. With the darkness, wind and snow it was impossible to tell what arrangements they had made for themselves, but I doubted that they were good. Sporadic shouting and flashes of head-torch light coming from their camp only reinforced that suspicion.

'I don't envy that pair,' I said to Sean, as I pulled the draw cord on the hood of my sleeping bag tight for the night.

I woke to bright sunlight. It was another fine morning, but it had obviously snowed heavily in the night. A snowdrift covered the foot of my bivouac bag and I kicked it away. Talk from the others drifted across. They did not sound happy.

'Good night, guys?' I asked.

'Bloody marvellous,' Tom said sarcastically. 'I can thoroughly recommend spending a night in an avalanche chute.'

We laughed at their misfortune, and it was only once I had moved across to their bivouac that I realised how awful it had been. They had been unable to find or dig out any sort of sheltered platform and in the end had settled for the open snow slope, but they soon hit ice. All they managed to excavate was a ledge big enough to sit on. At first this had been adequate, but as the storm worsened spindrift avalanches started pouring down from above, covering them in snow and pushing them off the platform. It had been necessary to unzip their bivouac bags and to dig the snow away every few minutes. Not only had they had a sleepless night, but a cold and damp one, as a lot of snow had got inside their sleeping bags.

'Tom got very wet,' Andy confided in me. 'He's a bit done in.'

'We'll go in front for a while. Maybe you'll be able to dry the sleeping bags while you wait on the stances.'

I waded back out to the ridge and began climbing up again. Progress had become very slow the previous day, but now it was virtually impossible. Nearly a metre of sugary snow was lying on top of ice. The snow simply slid away each time you tried to move up. After half an hour I had only moved about ten metres.

'Sorry about this,' I yelled down, but the others did not seem concerned with my lack of progress. They sat happily on foam mats soaking up the morning sun, their sleeping bags draped over their shoulders to allow them to dry.

As the snow steepened, steps would no longer take my weight. I began digging and found that once the ice below was exposed it was possible to move up on that. With painstaking slowness I moved up the ridge. However, once I had moved a few metres, the snow I had chopped away no longer piled up beneath me, but slid down the trench below and out of the bottom. I began to move faster, hacking away the snow in front with the shaft of my ice-axe thrust horizontally into the slope, while balancing on the front points of my crampons in the ice. The technique was tiring, but at least I was moving again.

'Looks like hard work,' Sean said when he arrived at the stance after I had finished the pitch.

'Got any better ideas?' I asked. He shook his head.

Sean climbed above me and I moved to the side of the trench to get out of the way of the snow pouring down, which made a hissing sound as it passed. The others followed behind and we inched our way towards the top. I hoped that the snow conditions would improve, but they did not. We dug all day.

After eight rope-lengths, over four hundred metres of trench lay below. Just as the sun was setting, I pulled on to a flat area at the side of a block of rock that formed the summit and proudly secured myself to it. Then I quickly dragged up the slack rope from below and prepared to belay Sean as he climbed up to join me.

A smile spread across my face. I had imagined this moment for over a year and now suddenly the reality seemed amusing. It felt good to reach the top, but the way in which we had done it was more satisfying. We could have planned our route more thoroughly and carried loads to the foot of the mountain before starting. Then we could have fixed a line of ropes some way up the peak and established a camp from which to climb higher. Any combination of these methods, while more time-consuming, would have given a greater chance of success. Instead, we had opted for a pure and simple approach and it had worked.

Besides the physical exertion in a wonderful outdoor setting, what had attracted me to climbing was that it did not have a strictly enforced set of rules. Individuals or groups of people choose how they are going to pursue the sport and there are no referees or judges presiding over what you do. It has always struck me as ironic that many pastimes people participate in during their spare time have sets of rules every bit as hierarchical and complex as those that govern their everyday lives.

As I got more involved in climbing I found out that people do follow unwritten ethical codes and that there are numerical systems for grading the difficulty of climbs. There are techniques and aids that are considered good practice and others that are not. Ultimately however, assuming climbers do not use very outmoded techniques or cause environmental damage, they will not come in for any criticism from their peers. What is considered unforgivable is to lie about the difficulty, position or techniques used on a particular climb.

We had set ourselves a difficult challenge to reach the top of Leyla Peak in the style we had chosen, but that was why I felt so happy with our ascent.

The sun continued to drop behind countless peaks across the border in India. There were so many that I could put names only to a handful of them. Then there was a lull in the wind as the first stars appeared. I was getting cold when Sean came over the top. He was smiling.

'Good one,' he said.

He was soon followed by Andy, who had tied on to the rope Sean was trailing. He did not look happy.

'Tom's fucked,' he announced.

The statement snapped me back to reality. We were in a very exposed position, on top of a big mountain with a cold night approaching.

'I'll see if there's a good spot to dig a snow hole,' I said moving up next to the summit block.

A bank of snow looked promising and I had just started to dig into it when Tom arrived. He looked washed out and hardly spoke. He simply came across to me and slumped down in the snow.

'Very tired,' was all he could say.

The others joined me and we took it in turns to enlarge the snow cave. After half an hour Andy announced it was big enough to fit us all in and we handed him his kit. Soon Sean was inside as well.

'Come on Tom,' I pleaded. 'Get inside the snow hole.' It was now getting very cold.

'I can't be bothered,' he replied. 'My sleeping bag is soaking wet. I might as well sit here. You go in. I'll be okay.'

'Tom,' I said sternly. 'Get in the hole.'

Tom pulled himself upright and I helped him remove his rucksack and harness. Then he slowly crawled to the entrance of the snow hole and slid inside, where Andy and Sean pushed him into his sleeping bag.

The snow cave was small and cramped. I slept fitfully and it seemed that whenever I woke, Tom's teeth were chattering. It was a relief when light started to filter in through the entrance tunnel. Once we saw sunlight we slipped outside.

It was a beautiful day. We basked in the sunshine, climbed on to the block that formed the summit and took some photographs. The top third of K2 stood prominently in the background. Then we scratched our names on to an empty gas cylinder and wedged it into a crack in the rock. It seemed a fitting way to mark our ascent. Afterwards we made hot drinks and lounged around drying our sleeping bags and clothing. The worries of the previous night drifted away.

'Are we going to go down?' Tom asked. 'Or shall we sit here all day?' It was eleven o'clock.

'It is very nice, but I guess we should go,' I replied.

We packed and I walked down from the summit block on the opposite side of the mountain to the one we had climbed up. After about ten metres there was a notch on the ridge. I peered over and stood back sharply.

'God it's steep down there.'

Below there was an overhanging rock wall that led down to some broken ground above a col. From the col a long couloir dropped off out of sight into the valley we had walked up to the foot of the climb. I knelt down, chopped the snow away from a protruding lump of rock and soon exposed a crack. I slid a nut into the crack and tapped it down with my axe. It would make a fine anchor for abseiling.

Once the abseil was prepared I slipped my descender on to the rope, clipped it to my harness and stepped over the side. The exposure made me giddy, but I slid down the ropes, spinning one way then the other. When only a few metres of rope remained beneath me I inspected the rock and found a small niche with some cracks in the back. I swung in, grabbed one of the cracks, placed a nut inside it and then clipped myself to it. Then I quickly backed up the anchor with several more, before unclipping from the rope and shouting up for the others to follow.

With four at the belay, it was very cramped. This struck me as amusing considering that we were surrounded by so much space. We could only move one at a time and it was a struggle to attach my descender to the ropes and slide away from the knot of bodies. But the abseils soon became routine and I began to relax when the steep wall ended on a snow slope. I stamped out a ledge and enjoyed the feeling of blood returning to my legs, after hanging in my harness for so long. Then I lazily placed a single nut into the rock above, clipped to it and yelled up to the others.

I looked down below. A few abseils across snow slopes and short rock walls led to another steep drop down to the col. It was close now. Then I heard a scream, faint at first, but immediately becoming louder. I looked up. Tom was coming down, but something was wrong. He was holding the rope with his hands and so should have been controlling the descender, but he appeared to be in free fall.

'Stop,' I shouted feebly. It was all I could think of doing.

Tom's plummet continued and I braced myself for his impact. Then he suddenly jerked to a halt just above me.

'Gloves are a bit icy,' he explained coolly.

Tom abseiled down the remaining rope with exaggerated care and landed in the snow next to me.

'You were lucky there,' I said. 'I'd not got hold of the ropes.'

On reaching a belay I usually began threading the ropes ready for the next abseil, and under such circumstances I might have been able to stop his fall. 'A little further and you'd have gone straight off the end of them.'

'Another life used up,' he said casually.

'How many left?'

'Oh, minus two at the last count.'

We smiled at each other and then laughed. We had put ourselves in this risky environment. Accepting and dealing with the dangers and challenges was all part of the excitement. Tom would be a little more careful, but he was not going to dwell too heavily on his near miss.

Two hours later we all stood on the col looking down the couloir. It seemed straightforward. The snow was at a reasonable angle. It was just a matter of down-climbing and if we reached some steep steps lower down we could always get out the ropes and abseil again.

I set off down the slope, facing in, swinging my feet and axes alternately, methodically climbing in reverse. After an initial steep section I turned to face outwards. Tom was just behind me.

'You know what?' I said. 'This looks the perfect angle for a ...' I sat down on my backside and pushed off. 'Bum slide.'

I quickly gathered speed and screamed. Sometimes I braked by thrusting my axes into the snow and at others I pushed with them to keep myself moving. With shrieks of joy I found that the height dropped away, and as the angle eased we stood up and skied on our plastic boots down the remaining snow. When the snow ended in a rubble-strewn gully we sat breathless, but still laughing. We had come down over 1,000 metres in half an hour.

The walk down the gully and into the main valley seemed an anticlimax, but I was pleased at how easily we had got off the mountain. Our plan had been loose and flexible and as a result we had continually been presented with choices. That made the climbing interesting and the outcome uncertain.

We had overcome the physical and technical challenges of the climbing, but to me the mental side of the climb was more satisfying. In the end our choice of tactics had been near perfect.

That night we stopped at a group of shepherds' huts on the trail back to base camp and shared a simple meal with a family watching over a herd of cattle. Their warmth and hospitality was overwhelming after six nights in the mountains and I soon felt guilty about how little conversation and entertainment we were providing in return. They asked about Leyla Peak and smiled when we signalled we had reached the top. We were so tired that for most of the evening we simply sat around the hearth, staring into the flames of the fire, before retiring early to a night on the roof-top under the stars.

Our cook Javed could barely contain his excitement when we arrived back in camp the following morning. He ran out of his tent into the small clearing to greet us, hugging everyone in turn.

'You climb Leyla Peak,' he stated.

'How did you know?'

'Two friends hunting ibex saw you with binoculars.'

I laughed. The upper sections of the valleys above Hushe village were only occasionally visited by locals, but obviously very little escaped their attention.

We all ducked under the tarpaulin we had set up as a kitchen and dining room and Javed lit the stove.

'What have you been doing Javed?' Andy asked.

'Very boring here, so I go to Hushe. Then I hear you climb Leyla Peak. I am very happy for you and I come back.'

Although earlier on in the trip Javed had expressed his own dislike of mountaineering, our achievement had pleased him. As a young man he had worked as a high altitude porter, carrying loads for mountaineering expeditions on K2. He had not enjoyed the work and despite the lower rates of pay and longer hours he switched to becoming a cook, a job involving less hardship and risk.

Talking to Javed and other villagers I had learned of the

hardships of their lives, of how children and the old died from sickness that could easily be treated with modern drugs, and women died in childbirth for want of hospital facilities. And then there were accidents. It seemed that villagers were regularly swept away by rivers, mudslides and avalanches, while some simply fell from high mountain paths.

I often wondered what the villagers thought of us. For them life was a dangerous struggle anyway, without setting artificially risky challenges for themselves. For that reason most people seemed to stay out of the higher mountains. It must have seemed at best decadent, and at worst insane that we had come from the other side of the world to attempt to climb mountains that they themselves dismissed as places to be avoided.

And yet that was not the case. Javed was genuinely delighted by our climb, which had been the first ascent of the mountain.

'This climb harder than K2, I think,' he said proudly from behind his roaring stoves.

I wondered why he was so pleased for us. I knew he could understand the physical hardship we had been through and the danger we had faced, but I got the impression the admiration went further than that. I knew the local people had been flattered by our interest in their lives and the place in which they lived. We had after all, chosen to visit this particular valley, out of the many thousands of valleys across the Karakoram. But I think they also respected the fact that we had come for a purpose, other than to just look. There was also a pure mercenary element that the pleasure our climbing of Leyla Peak brought to the villagers. We had employed many people and spent money in the village shops. If we were encouraged, perhaps we would return and bring others.

I knew that historically people had traded and travelled throughout the mountains and higher up we had seen recently abandoned shepherds' huts. It appeared the locals were moving out of the mountains and their visits were becoming less frequent. Perhaps, with improving roads and increasing wealth it was no longer necessary to trade or farm in these remote areas, or people were simply moving out to take up better opportunities elsewhere. Yet a great bond with the mountains still remained. This land was their home. By venturing into this wilderness I felt we were looked upon as embracing a part of their culture that was being lost, which only added to the respect we were shown.

'Lunch ready,' Javed called from the kitchen shelter, banging on a saucepan lid. We shuffled back to the tarpaulin, having drifted away to unpack and dry our damp gear.

Javed had excelled himself. There were eggs, parathas and chips – difficult and time-consuming to make on the kerosene stove. We ate the meal greedily, which finished with a water melon carried up from the village. It was a typically kind gesture.

'Still not eating?' Andy asked Javed at the end of the meal. He shook his head. He was observing the Moslem fast of Ramadan and from sunrise to sunset ate and drank nothing. He even smoked cigarettes from between his cupped fingers so that they did not touch his lips. Yet despite Javed's fasting he spent nearly all day preparing food for us. Although we all respected what he was doing, it was difficult to resist having a joke at his expense.

In the evening before our dinner, Javed prepared his own food. Then, as it started to get dark, he turned on his radio. He listened intently to a station broadcasting from Skardu, the regional capital. We had learned to recognise the shrill tones of the mullah who read a sermon just before the fast could be broken.

'What is he saying?' Tom asked.

'He says, "God is great."'

'Didn't he say that the other night?'

'Yes.'

As soon as the sermon ended Javed drank two cups of tea in quick succession and started shovelling rice into his mouth.

'Weather,' he announced earnestly through mouthfuls of food, concentrating hard on the radio.

(*Above*) Alan Wilkie in Snell's Field, Chamonix, France

(*Left*) Joe Simpson on the North Face of the Aiguille Blanc de Peuterey, Italy.

(*Below*) Looking down on John Silvester climbing the Second Icefield on the North Face of the Eiger, Switzerland.

(*Above*) John Silvester on the summit ridge of the Eiger.

(*Left*) Leyla Peak, northern Pakistan. We climbed up to a gully to breach the rock band in the bottom right of the picture, before moving back left to join the snow ridge.

(*Below*) Looking up at Tom Curtis and Andy Cav tackling the gully on Leyla Peak.

(*Left*) On the summit of Leyla Peak - Simon, Tom Curtis, Andy Cave and Sean Smith.

(*Right*) Mark Miller in front of the damaged Leicester University Jeep, Pakistan.

(*Left*) The Biale Expedition at base camp. Standing: captain Naveed, our liaison officer, Sean Smith, Nick Groves, Simon and Mary Rose Fowlie. Sitting: Mike Searle, Mark Miller and Haqeem, our cook.

(*Right*) The South Face of Biale. We climbed diagonally leftwards from the basin to the snowy col and then followed the ridge above.

(*Left*) Nick Groves climbing high on Lobsang II. Mustagh Tower and K2 are behind.

(*Below*) Sean Smith reaching the col on Biale. Behind are K2 Mustagh Tower, Broad Peak, Gasherbrum IV and Gasherbrum I.

(*Bottom*) Looking west from th col at the Great Trango Tower and Nameless Tower, with Uli Biaho behind.

(*Left*) Typical country in the foothills of eastern Nepal.

(*Right*) Anne Murray below the south face of Kanchenjunga after our epic trek through the jungle.

(*Left*) Ruined temple in Hampi, India.

(*Right*) Anne's motorbike in a small northern Thai village.

Joe Simpson re-enacting our Peruvian drama for American TV in the Bugaboos, Canadian Rockies.

Kevin tends to his truck crossing the Nullabor Plain, Australia.

(*Left*) Simon rock climbing at Mount Arapiles, Victoria, Australia.

(*Below*) Simon and Sean Smith admiring the fields of Nagar on the walk in to the Hispar, northern Pakistan.

(*Right*) Access work on the Broadgate Development, London.

(*Above*) Guiding in Scotland. The aftermath of the minibus crash.

(*Left*) Our Christmas tree at Nanga Parbat base camp, northern Pakistan. The tangerines were frozen solid.

(*Below*) Arbat Street, Moscow.

(*Above*) Khan Tengri above the International Camp, Soviet Kazakhstan.

(*Left*) Members of the Russ[ian] National Mountaineering Squad sunbathing at base ca[mp] after a storm.

(*Below left*) Near the summ[it] of Khan Tengri.

(*Below right*) Simon on the summit of Khan Tengri.

'What is it?' we pleaded.

'He says . . . some good . . . some bad.'

We burst into laughter. The forecast had been the same every evening we listened to it.

In the morning after breakfast we helped Andy pack, then divided up his belongings and set off down to Hushe. Andy was keen to leave as soon as possible, to travel on to Nepal and climb with some other friends there. We wanted to see him off, and reasoned that a rest in the village would do us good before attempting another mountain.

I walked down in a haze, marvelling at the barren hillsides running up to patches of green below the mountains far above. Lower down it was drier, with few plants. The sparsely spaced trees had all been cropped by the villagers for firewood. Then suddenly we rounded a corner and entered fields on the edge of the village. The contrast was staggering. Everywhere was green and reeked of life. Higher up there had been hardly any smells and now the air was full of them.

The tiny fields of wheat, potatoes and peas, irrigated by thin water channels, were lined with fragrant grasses and flowers. The water bubbled along the channels, below walls and across paths. Men waved at us from the fields and we watched as they carefully added and removed stones to switch water from one channel to another. The village was an oasis of green in a landscape that was now all greys and browns.

Just before we reached the houses, we met a group of western trekkers. We said hello, but did not talk to them for long. I felt uneasy after weeks of relative isolation and soon decided we had little in common. We walked on into the village, greeting people whom we had met before. Javed directed us to a room separate from his own house and we sat inside as children gathered around the windows. It was nice to feel so welcome.

Soon Javed returned with a thermos full of tea and a plate of parathas.

'You want turnip, or turniptop curry for dinner?' he asked. It had already become a staple as the only fresh vegetable available and none was wasted. The leaves were similar to spinach.

'Let's have a treat,' I replied. 'We'll have both together.'

Javed looked sternly at me. We had not had the dish before. He went away in silence and I wondered if he would agree to my request. When the food arrived, the roots and leaves had been mixed. Javed had even found some fresh yoghurt to supplement the meal. It tasted wonderful.

As the light began to fade, children left us alone and the village fell silent. Without an electricity supply people simply went to bed not long after it got dark. We stayed up later than most, playing several hands of bridge, but were still tired from the climb and so were bedded down by eight in the evening. After the continual activity of the previous week I was relishing a night of uninterrupted sleep with a roof over our heads, and fell asleep almost immediately.

When I woke there was noise and confusion and it was still dark. Someone was yelling and I soon noticed itchy lumps all over my skin.

'You little bastards,' I heard Tom shout. He was hitting something repeatedly.

'Calm down Tom,' Sean said.

I reached for my head torch and turned it on. Tom was crawling around on his hands and knees wearing just his underpants hitting the floor with a leather boot.

'What's the matter?' I asked.

'Bloody bedbugs,' he replied without interrupting the blows.

I turned the torch on my own body and saw bites everywhere. Then I noticed flat brown insects crawling down the walls. They were almost as big as ladybirds. Others were dropping off the ceiling. I inspected my sleeping bag. There were lots of them inside. Little splashes of blood lay around the bugs Tom had already squashed.

'Bed beetles more like,' Andy observed, joining in the swatting.

By burning candles and leaving our torches on, we stemmed

the flow of the insects, but the night became a sleepless ordeal. Whenever I closed my eyes I started itching and imagined my sleeping bag crawling with them.

We spent a further anxious night in Javed's house before Andy managed to get on a jeep to Skardu. The bedbugs must have been full because they hardly bit. Nevertheless, it was a relief to leave and return to the camp.

Tom was running out of time before he was due to make his way home. In a frenzy of activity we completed the first ascent of Nemeka, another beautiful mountain nearby. We simply packed our rucksacks and set off the day after we returned from Hushe. After approaching the peak from a valley we had not even looked into before, we descended blind into another valley after reaching the summit. In many ways this made the climb even more of an adventure than our ascent of Leyla Peak. But for me both were deeply satisfying experiences and I felt as if I was coming of age as a mountaineer.

Finally, after Tom had gone home, Sean and I stayed on alone at the base camp and after a few days' rest tried to climb one more peak. My strength seemed to have finally depleted after weeks of continuous dysentery. I found walking to the mountain a struggle and on the second day I was nearly washed away while trying to cross a glacial river. The shock of my narrow escape and the bitterly cold water were too much for my weary body. For over an hour I sat on a pile of stones at the side of the river, shivering and occasionally convulsing. There were moments when I thought my body would never warm again. We did carry on, taking a diversion on to the glacier to avoid the river crossing, but the following day I felt too weak to continue. I wearily made my way back to the base camp, where we broke camp and then staggered back down to the village under the weight of enormous rucksacks. But despite the final failure, the trip had been an overwhelming success. We caught a jeep back to Skardu and began the long journey by road back down the Karakoram Highway.

In Rawalpindi Sean set about acquiring a Chinese visa. He

planned to travel back up the Highway, cross into China and ultimately to traverse Tibet. I hung around for a few days, paralysed by the thought of returning to Britain. Without a job or a home to return to and little idea of what I would do next, there seemed little purpose to going back. At least here in Pakistan on a mountaineering expedition life was fresh and exciting. But in the end I could delay my departure no longer.

We parted with a feeble handshake outside our hotel. It seemed sad after all we had been through. I dearly wanted to stay and travel with Sean, but did not have enough money. Although I had never been away with him before, I had spent much time in Sean's company. We had been to college together and had shared a house, so it was hardly surprising we had become close during the expedition. So close that during the days we spent together at the end of the trip we had hardly spoken. There was little need to, as we both knew what the other was thinking. Now we would not see each other for many months.

'I'll see you when you get back,' I said sadly from the window of the taxi. 'Have a good time.'

'Yeah, sure. Count me in for the next trip,' I heard Sean say as the car jolted out into the stream of traffic, heading for the railway station.

In Karachi I was dismayed to find the next flight home I could catch was in five days' time. I had very little money left and had hoped for an earlier flight. I booked myself into a very cheap hotel by the railway station and worked out my budget. I could afford a vegetable curry and two chappattis for each evening meal, with one rupee left over to barter for bananas for the rest of the day's food. There was no money for bottled water or cold drinks. I reckoned the little spare money left over would cover a bus to the airport.

Fortunately I did not feel very hungry. My dysentery was so severe that any food I ate quickly gave me stomach cramps and bad wind. Then it passed straight through me and came out mixed with blood and mucus. A typical day passed bartering for bananas, sleeping and visiting the toilet. Sometimes I felt strong enough to go for a short walk.

It was a great relief finally to get on the plane home, although the airline food upset my stomach even more. I spent most of the flight either inside the toilet, or queuing outside, willing the occupant to get a move on.

As I walked through the green channel at customs back at Heathrow, I was stopped. The officers were not impressed with my filthy clothes and gaunt thin appearance and took a particular interest in the series of three flea bites running up a vein on my left arm. After searching my bags they led me into a bare white room with one plastic chair chained to the floor in the corner and strip-searched me.

Chapter Four

At Home Abroad

I paced around the hospital room restlessly, before stopping at the window and staring outside. The sky was grey and drab, which matched the room and my mood. It was the last place I wanted to be.

I had been back from Pakistan only three days. I did not feel particularly ill and saw my continuing diarrhoea as more of an inconvenience than a serious problem. During the time away I had gradually lost weight, but viewed my emaciated body as being lean and fit. My parents, however, did not and insisted that I go to hospital. A doctor made a cursory examination of a stool sample, weighed me and promptly admitted me. I had arrived back in the country with just twenty-two pence to my name and now I had been incarcerated in hospital. All my fears about coming back to Britain seemed well founded.

My situation depressed me. I had been free, travelling and climbing in a far-away country just the week before and now I was trapped. The doctors had little idea of what was wrong with me or how to treat me, and simply said I should stay while they completed their tests. I was given a bedpan and every time I used it, I had to press an alarm. A nurse would come and inspect the contents and write the results on a form on the door. When my family and friends visited for the first time they had to wear paper clothes and face masks. It felt as if I was in prison.

On the second day a doctor appeared, whom I had not seen before.

'I'd just like to take a blood sample Mr Yates,' he said.

I looked away as he put a tourniquet around my upper left arm and began to probe at my veins lower down. He stabbed the needle in and pulled it out several times.

'Careful,' I pleaded. 'That hurts.'

'Sorry, can't seem to find a vein.'

I found his excuse hard to take. My body was covered in bulging veins. In addition to those normally visible, they were sticking out of my legs and even my stomach.

'Just try the other side,' he said, after further probing.

All the poking with the needle started to make me feel faint. Eventually he withdrew the needle. The syringe had only a little blood inside.

'That'll have to do,' he said, taking the sample away.

Within half an hour bruises had run up and down both arms from my elbows and I could barely move them. The doctor returned and seemed undeterred by the damage he had done.

'We'll have to do some more tests,' he announced. 'You wouldn't mind if we brought in some medical students, would you? They rarely get the chance to examine someone so thin.'

Over the following two days I was subjected to a variety of painful, uncomfortable and degrading tests. Pipes were put into me from either end. Samples were removed from my intestine and my colon. I ate a slab of butter and blood samples were taken at half-hourly intervals to gauge my rate of fat absorption. The students visited, prodded me about and got very excited about feeling the outline of my heart under my rib-cage. I sat through the tests passively, although I did begin to feel increasingly hungry with the inadequate hospital food.

'Could I have some more?' I asked a nurse after the third evening meal.

'I'll see what I can do,' she replied kindly.

A little later she returned with two spare portions of rhubarb crumble. I ate them greedily. They went straight through me and within two hours I was using the bedpan and ringing the alarm at regular intervals. It was a long and weary night and yet I still looked forward to the breakfast trolley arriving in the morning.

When breakfast did arrive, I was given a drink and nothing more. The trolley was taken away and after a while I realised I was not going to be fed. The same happened at lunch. I began to get incredibly hungry and yet still did not ask why I had been given no food.

At dinner the trolley passed me by yet again. I had had enough. I felt angry for willingly handing over responsibility for myself to the hospital staff, for slipping so easily and unquestionably into the role of the patient. Just a couple of weeks before I had been making life or death decisions for myself, and now I had happily surrendered to others the basic decision of whether to eat or not.

I stormed out of my room and up the ward wearing just a pair of pyjama bottoms. I spotted some staff through a window in a side room and burst in through the door.

'Look at me,' I pleaded, pointing at my protruding ribs. 'I'm a bag of bones, and for some reason you lot have decided to starve me.'

The doctors and nurses looked stunned, but for a moment were speechless.

'Mr Yates, we are in the middle of a meeting,' a nurse finally said. 'We will come and see you in a minute.'

I returned to my room still fuming, wondering why we bow to authority and allow ourselves to become institutionalised so unquestioningly. It seemed ridiculous that the urge to herd, not to cause a fuss and not to stand out could at times be strong enough to override the basic need to eat.

After a short time the ward sister came into my room.

'We stopped feeding you because of your reaction to the extra puddings,' she explained.

'It would have been nice to have been told,' I pointed out.

'I'll see what I can do about getting you some food,' she replied sympathetically, before leaving.

A little later the sister returned with some sandwiches, and for the rest of my stay I was given double helpings at mealtimes regardless of their effect.

In the morning the doctor proudly announced to me that the tests showed I had dysentery. It was information I had known for two months.

After five days I was discharged from hospital with a handful of antibiotics, the same I had been taking all summer with little effect. I had blindly followed the advice of those around me, been their guinea pig and undergone a variety of painful tests for nothing. It was over a year later before my digestive system returned to normal. As I left I realised that I could have bought the same tablets from a pharmacy in Rawalpindi a little over a week earlier for just a few rupees and prevented the nightmare of the previous few days.

I looked across the table at Mike, who seemed to be getting increasingly anxious as the meal went on. Mike Searle was a quietly spoken academic and it was rare to see him getting particularly bothered by anything. I had made my first trip to Pakistan with him two years previously. Having suggested that we return to try an unclimbed peak called Biale that he had found, he had taken it upon himself to organise much of the expedition. In addition to Sean, Mark Miller and myself he had invited along his longstanding friend Nick Groves and his partner Mary Rose Fowlie. At times I wondered if he ever doubted his choice of climbing companions.

'I'm beginning to get worried about Mark,' he said. 'He should have brought the jeep back over an hour ago.'

'The what?' spluttered Sean.

'The jeep. I let him go to Islamabad in it.'

Sean and I burst out laughing.

'But he can't drive, Mike,' Sean pointed out. 'Well he can sort of, but he's never taken a test.'

'Oh, dear,' said Mike, now looking very worried. 'He didn't tell me he hadn't got a licence.'

'Well he wouldn't, would he?' Sean replied casually.

'I'm sure he'll be all right,' I said trying to reassure him. 'He's probably just gone to visit some friends.'

We continued the meal in a tense silence and I tried to exude an air of confidence I did not have. Strange events had a habit of happening in Mark's vicinity.

Then suddenly Mark burst in through the restaurant door. He was red-faced, sweating heavily and covered in dirt and oil. He stormed up to our table.

'I've rolled the jeep,' he announced, sitting down and grabbing the jug of water. He drank two glasses in succession, before adding, 'But don't worry, I've had it fixed.'

The colour completely drained from Mike's face. I was not surprised. The precious jeep belonged to Leicester University, his employers, and had been specially shipped out to Pakistan for a geology project they were running in the country.

'Where is it now?' Mike asked feebly.

'Outside.'

The pair went off to look at the damage, while we continued with the meal. Mike came back a little later.

'I'm sorry, but I'm going to have to take the jeep to a garage.'

'I thought Mark had fixed it,' Sean quipped.

'Well I think it needs looking over.'

'We'd better go and check it out,' I said, putting down my chappatti and heading for the door.

The jeep was parked across the main road down a side street, where there was no lighting. At first sight little seemed to be wrong, but Mike quickly started pointing out faults. There were scratches down one side, the bonnet was buckled and the doors protruded from their surrounds. Mark had obviously parked it in the gloom to try to hide the damage.

'Hey, look at this, guys,' shouted Sean.

He was standing in front of the jeep looking at it head on. I saw the problem as soon as I joined him. The entire vehicle was lopsided. Sean and I began to giggle.

'So tell me again. What happened?' Mike demanded angrily.

I let most of Mark's story pass me by. The crux seemed to involve a thunderstorm and a bullock cart, but as it had been dry and sunny all day where we were, a mere twenty kilometres away, the story sounded implausible. I remembered an elaborate tale Mark had told me some months earlier back in Sheffield, concerning the loss of my cycle, which I had lent to him. I later learned a more truthful version of events. He had simply left it unlocked outside a shop and it had been stolen.

Fortunately, the jeep did start and Mike and Mark went off in search of a garage. We returned to the restaurant and finished the meal. When they arrived back at the hotel later that night, Mike said an additional problem had been discovered – the bolts holding the engine in place had all sheared in the accident. Had they not been replaced, the engine could have dropped out on to the road at any time.

We had hoped to leave for the mountains the following day, but it seemed as if events were conspiring against us. The jeep had to be taken for repairs and we were still short of a liaison officer. We had paid a peak fee for the mountain we wished to climb, and the Ministry of Tourism regulations stipulated that the expedition had to be accompanied by a liaison officer.

When we had arrived a few days before and met the officials in the Ministry, we were told they were expecting us a week later. Mike protested that he had written saying we were arriving early. They retrieved the expedition file from a dusty cabinet and soon found the letter. It was evident that nobody had even bothered to read it. However, despite their mistake, we were not allowed to leave for the mountains without the officer.

Mike and I stepped out of the taxi and into the manicured gardens outside the Ministry of Tourism offices in Islamabad. We walked into the now familiar office with its tatty pictures of K2 on the walls and a creaking fan on the ceiling, and sat down.

'Where's our liaison officer?' I demanded from the official behind the desk.

'He has been summoned from Lahore and should arrive presently.'

'You said that yesterday. When is he going to arrive?'

'Maybe today, perhaps tomorrow.'

'I'm getting pissed off with this,' I said to Mike. 'We want our liaison officer now,' I shouted. 'Do you understand?'

'Do you have a wife, Mr Simon?'

'No,' I replied puzzled.

'Well, this is why you are so anxious,' the official explained. 'If you were to get yourself a wife, then you would be much more content.'

'But I don't want a wife,' I replied trying to stop a smile from breaking across my face. It was difficult to counter his simple logic, and Mike was already laughing openly. 'I just want a liaison officer.'

A day later when we arrived at the Ministry we were greeted by a fresh-faced young army captain called Naveed. The official proudly announced that the government of Pakistan had allocated him to our expedition as liaison officer. We sat through the formality of a briefing and were then allowed to leave for the mountains. Sean cannily arranged a lift with Mike in the jeep, under the pretext that he would be able to take photographs on the way. We filled the back of the jeep with baggage.

'Well, I'm afraid the rest of you will have to get on the bus,' Mike announced.

'Oh, right,' Mark remarked, raising an eyebrow.

'Well, Mike's hardly going to let you share the driving. Is he?' I said cynically.

'I suppose not,' he was forced to admit.

Reluctantly, we took a taxi to the bus station and booked some seats for a night coach to Gilgit.

Three days later we sat in the gardens of the K2 Motel

in Skardu, drinking tea. The setting could hardly have been grander. The town lay in the centre of a flood plain, where the Indus river spilled out of the mountains and meandered sluggishly, before pouring down into a gorge cutting into the foothills. The hotel itself stood on a terrace high above a broad bend in the river, overlooked by an old fort perched on a rocky hill. The views out across the river and into the distant Shigar valley were superb and it was just possible to make out tantalising outlines of snow-capped peaks on the horizon.

'I've been thinking,' said Mark.

'Oh dear,' replied Mike laughing.

'What do you think about Simon and I going on ahead and finding a spot to put the base camp?'

'That's not a bad idea. If we arrange a place to meet you can guide us to the site you have chosen.'

Mark's suggestion was sensible as we had very little information about the approaches to the mountain. In fact our knowledge was limited to some distant photographs Mike had taken a few years earlier and a notoriously inaccurate map.

When two days later, Mark and I got out of the jeep beyond the small village of Dassu, it was something of a shock. It felt unnatural to be saying goodbye at the start of the trip, even if the parting was only temporary. I was looking forward to getting into the mountains though and getting some exercise after the days of cramped travel. Unlike the others we would be able to move quickly without the burden of dozens of porters and the associated starts, stops and continual negotiations.

'We'll see you in ten days' time, at the junction of the Trango and Baltoro Glaciers,' said Mike.

'Right,' I replied, delighted by the vagueness of the meeting arrangements. We were talking about a vast area of glacier and yet I had no doubt that we would meet as planned. We simply had to, otherwise we would run out of food. We shook hands, shouldered our rucksacks and walked across the small landslide blocking the road towards a baked brown gorge.

When I reached the other side of the debris I looked back. Mike had already turned the jeep round and was driving away from us down the thin dirt road.

Walking over the jumble of large brown boulders required intense concentration. They had a slippery, shiny finish, as if the outer rock had been melted by the searing sunlight. To cross the large chasms between the stones often required a jump. A mistake could easily result in a leg-breaking fall.

I skipped across the rocks trying to catch glimpses of Mark's unmistakably large frame through the heat haze in front. It was difficult to keep up with his pace and the sun, dry air and warm wind was desiccating my body. I could feel the salt from dried sweat in my clothes chafing my skin. Our three days of walking had been much the same. A very early start followed by flat-out marching with minimal rests until the early afternoon. This way we could cover a good distance and then set up camp to escape the hottest part of the day.

Suddenly the boulder field ended. For hours we had been walking steadily uphill, now there was just a thin dusty path contouring across a scrubby hillside. Huge granite cliffs hung above, which made my neck ache when I tried to look at them.

I turned a corner and the view changed, but I kept walking until the picture was complete. About a kilometre further up the valley at the base of the cliffs a ribbon of radiant green ran down the hillside. Some large birch trees stuck into the air and their leaves shimmered silver in the wind. Locals called the place Paiju. Beyond the green the valley opened out. I could see the snout of the Baltoro Glacier and a highway of ice beyond it. Spectacular mountains stood on either side.

As I entered the oasis I could see that springs rising at the base of the cliffs provided the water, which ran downhill in small streams. Below the birch trees were more abundant willows and roses. The ground was covered in grass and flowers. Insects and butterflies filled the air. Bird song echoed all around and a rich smell of life hung about the place.

It was, however, a flawed paradise used as a campsite by many on their way to K2 or the other peaks along the Baltoro Glacier. Large terraces had been chopped into the earth for tent platforms, and many were covered in rubbish. Porters from many expeditions were tearing at the undergrowth for firewood and there was a distinct smell of excrement. Yet despite the faults Paiju was still a unique and special place.

Mark had found a decent platform in the centre of the site and was already setting up the tent. Anwar was busy with the stove nearby. It was the first time I had seen him for a few hours, as it had proved impossible to keep up with him. I had met Anwar Ali briefly the year before in Hushe and on the back of his wicked sense of humour had offered him work the next time I returned to Pakistan. We had hired him to act as both porter and cook for our reconnaissance. He was already proving to be exceptional at both.

'Lunch ready,' he announced with a characteristic smile, handing Mark and me bowls of dhal and a plate full of freshly made chappattis.

'You're a star, Anwar,' Mark said as he eagerly began to eat. It was impossible to disagree with him. Anwar was carrying a larger load than either of us, faster, and he still had enough energy to start cooking the moment he arrived in camp.

Anwar watched us eat and insisted that we finished all he had prepared.

'What will you have?' Mark asked.

'I will go and see my friends,' Anwar replied.

He went and joined a group of about a dozen porters further down the hillside. Literally hundreds of people were at the campsite for the night and most were porters, who had split into groups for cooking and eating. People came from the whole of the north of Pakistan to work as porters on the Baltoro and usually formed clans based on which region or valley they came from.

A little later Anwar returned clutching something in his hands.

'Oh Anwar,' Mark groaned. 'That's gross.'

He smiled broadly, holding what I now recognised as a goat's head. The head was blackened and smooth from being burnt to remove the hair.

'Now I make goat's head soup,' Anwar proudly announced, putting the head into the pressure cooker. He added a little water and soon had the dish hissing over the stove. An hour later he opened the steaming pan and began eating the head. The neck and face went first, then Anwar gouged out the eyes, before cracking open the skull and starting on the brain.

'You're not a vegetarian then Anwar?' Mark asked jokingly, as he chewed away the gums from the jaw. Nothing was wasted and only bones and teeth remained.

The next morning we decided to have a rest day. The porters usually paused at Paiyu as it was the last camp before the glacier. I spent a lot of time watching them stock up with firewood and prepare bread, chappattis and parathas to cook higher up.

Anwar became friendly with a coach driver from Abbotabad, who had somehow ended up working as a cook for the liaison officer of a Yugoslav expedition that was going to K2. It turned out that he had never left the plains of Pakistan and had no idea about the place he now found himself. He was a lousy cook and was terrified by the prospect of going on to the glacier.

To me, his was a remarkable story, but in some ways just an extreme example of that of many of the men who were in Paiyu that day. Although most of those working as porters did come from mountain areas, many rarely left their small villages and most never ventured deep into the mountains themselves. Most would have endured days of travel by jeep, bus and foot to reach the villages where hiring took place. There was no guarantee of work at the end of their travels and competition for jobs was so fierce that men virtually fought over them. Nearly all the men would have left their villages with very limited supplies of food and money.

We had come to Pakistan to climb – a pastime that is considered in the western world to involve high levels of adventure and risk. Yet we had travelled in relative comfort and were bringing those comforts with us into the mountains. As I lay inside the tent in my warm down sleeping bag, reading before I went to sleep, I could see the porters settling down for the night under single blankets. They huddled together to keep warm. To me it seemed in many ways there was more uncertainty, risk and adventure in their work than in our mountaineering.

In the morning we left Paiyu. Once we were on to the glacier, the main track to Concordia and ultimately K2 Base Camp veered to the other side. For a while we followed a vague path on the north side of the glacier, but it quickly disappeared altogether, leaving us following Anwar as he picked his way through the rolling, rubble-covered ice. Eventually we reached the Trango glacier and crossed to its far side.

'This will do,' I said, dumping my rucksack on a mud flat next to a large glacial pool.

'We'll call it dust camp,' Mark joked. His face was already covered and as he stamped his feet clouds of the grey powder blew into the air.

In a bout of activity over two days, Mark and I explored the surrounding glacier systems, discovered a site for our Biale base camp and marvelled at the Trango Towers, some of the largest rock towers in the world. Then we returned to the camp to wait for the others. Mark gathered dust. Whatever he did he seemed to cover himself in more of the ash-like powder.

'You look like an aborigine doing one of those ceremonial dances,' I observed, sniggering.

After a day of waiting we were awoken early the next morning. The arrival of the others with twenty-three porters took us by surprise. We had expected them at the end of a day. We hurriedly got dressed and broke camp while Anwar made some tea for everyone. There was a tense atmosphere among the porters.

'There's been some trouble,' Sean explained. 'The porters are not happy about walking on this side of the glacier and they stopped yesterday after what they considered a full day's walk. They say they will not walk long today.'

There was one porter who seemed to be doing the talking.

'He's the guy who's been causing most of the trouble,' Sean continued. 'I nearly dobbed him yesterday.'

'Right, we'll have to sort him out,' I replied.

We set off at a blistering pace, but I was deeply worried about what the porters would do. We had limited funds and the porters were our largest expense by far. It looked as if they would stop short of the base camp we had chosen and demand more money to go on.

Sean and I isolated the ring-leader at the back of the group and tried to slow him down, while Mark continued at a relentless pace. Hours passed and the group got more spread out. After we crossed another side-glacier there were murmurings of discontent, and I noticed that Mike was beginning to march in front of the porters.

'What's Mike in a hurry for?' I asked Sean.

'He's got the money,' he replied smiling.

Once the porters knew their wages had gone off in front, they realised there was no point in delaying tactics. Even if they abandoned their loads, they would still have to catch Mike to collect their money. Further protest would simply delay their return.

Finally, over a crest on the ridge we had been following, the small grassy ablation valley that we had chosen for our base camp came into view. It was a very dramatic place. A small triangle of grass defined by moraine ridges on two sides and sweeping granite slabs on the other. Mike was already paying off the crowd of gathered porters.

'It's some spot this,' Mike remarked as the porters left.

Eventually the last man departed and there was silence. Our contact with the world outside was leaving. The remoteness of the place sank in immediately and the mountains seemed to gain in size. I felt exhilarated, but at the same time nervous. This was beyond anything I had experienced before. I hardly noticed the concern in Nick's voice as he helped our cook Haqeem sort out the loads.

'Shit,' he shouted, 'They've taken one load of flour and one load of rice.'

We had not managed to outwit the porters after all.

'Right. Let's do it,' said Mark dramatically.

Sean, Mark and myself were in a tent on a col between two of the Lobsang Spires. Having climbed up a couloir below in the night, we had paused for a brew and to let the coldest part of the night pass before starting the more technical climbing above. Now the sun was coming up, it was time to leave the tent.

There was little to do but put our plastic climbing boots back on again and get on with the climbing. As we expected to be back down later the same day, we could leave much of our kit behind in the tent.

'Have you seen my sunglasses?' Sean asked searching through his rucksack.

'No,' we chorused in reply.

'Does anyone have a spare pair?'

'Sorry.'

'I'm going to have to go down then.'

As Mark and I moved away from the tent towards Lobsang II, Sean began down-climbing the couloir. He looked despondent. There was little else he could do. A day exposed to the light reflecting from the snow and ice could easily send him snow blind. It did not seem appropriate to shout down goodbye.

Before Sean was out of sight, Mark was already climbing above. I sat and belayed, marvelling at how elegantly he was moving his large, powerful body up thin runnels of ice lying over steep rock slabs. He was having to place his ice-axes very delicately to avoid knocking away the ice. Mark was not always so careful. On many occasions I had struggled to follow him up ice-climbs he had knocked away.

Climbing with Mark was always fun though, even when it

was not going well. I remembered how when half way up a climb in Scotland we stopped to have a bite to eat and Mark clumsily pulled an apple out of the top pocket of his rucksack. As the apple flew out of his hands and down the face, I laughed. 'I've got an orange I can lose later,' he said casually. I forgot about the incident until he opened his rucksack again and the orange bounced out.

It was soon my turn to follow. The climbing was not overly difficult, but the position was sensational. Nearby the slabby face we were climbing ended in a ridge. The face beyond must have been very steep, because it was possible to look straight down to a glacier over a thousand metres below. The glacier led up to the shapely slopes of Mustagh Tower.

We climbed on until it seemed that Mark had arrived at the top.

'You're not going to believe this view,' he said as I climbed up just below him.

I took a photo of him astride a pinnacle of rock before joining him. In all directions there was nothing but mountains and glaciers. I gazed at the Baltoro Glacier. From up there it looked like an amazing patchwork of rubble and differing shades of green and blue pools lying on the ice. In front of us were four of the world's fourteen 8,000-metre peaks. K2, Broad Peak and the Gasherbrums I and II stood above countless other peaks of slightly smaller stature. Biale, the mountain we had come to climb, was nearby. They all looked breathtaking.

'Hey, we're not on the summit,' I pointed out.

'So what?' Mark replied.

I could see his point. A knife-edge ridge stretched out from where we were sitting for two hundred metres to a slightly higher pinnacle. It would have taken many hours to reach, besides it was nicer to just sit in the sun and take in the view.

We sat for far too long, simply staring.

'I'm getting addled,' Mark announced.

'Me too.'

Without another word we began setting up an abseil and then set off down.

By the time we arrived back at the col it was desperately hot. We simply dived into the tent with the others and sat in our underpants through the heat of the day.

Sean had met Mike and Nick coming up on his way down. Fortunately Mike had a spare pair of sunglasses, so Sean had been able to turn around and immediately come back up again.

In the late afternoon it had cooled enough for us to leave the others and descend the couloir. We paused briefly on the glacier to look at Biale and stash some gear under a large boulder before walking slowly back to the camp. The others returned the following day, Sean and Nick having climbed to the same high point as Mark and I, while Mike opted to wait for them at the col. They too had come to the conclusion that following the ridge further to gain a slightly higher summit was not worth the effort. We had only intended to climb the peak as a means of acclimatising, and as such, although we had not reached the top, the outing had been completely successful. Now it was time to turn our attention to the main objective.

I awoke to the shrill tone of a small plastic alarm clock next to my head. I still felt very sleepy. Turning on my head torch, I soon saw why – the clock read 11 p.m. I had been asleep for just three hours. I stopped the alarm and let out a deep sigh. It was a strange time to be starting a day's climbing.

Five unproductive days had passed since the climb on Lobsang. It had taken us two days to figure out the correct way up the glacier and through an ice-fall. After a day's rest, it had then taken a further two days to reach the bottom of the face. Above, we would follow a line of snowy ramps across the left-hand side of the face to reach a ridge. The ridge offered an interesting and safe line to the summit. The waist-deep wet snow on the glacier had convinced us that it would be best to operate at night, at least on the lower part of the mountain.

Silently we began our day. Having recently had an evening meal there was little for us to do. We had one drink each and then packed everything into our rucksacks. Outside was cold and clear and the ground below us was frozen. We collapsed the tent and then started. It was a joy to be able to stand on the snow without sinking into it.

We walked slowly across the frosty, high plateau in our solitary patches of head-torch light. It was hard to imagine that the same place had been a furnace during the day. After crossing the bergschrund we started climbing.

'Let's get rid of this rope,' Mark suggested, already untying from his end.

Now we were off the glacier there was little need for it. There was no danger of falling into a crevasse and we would move together up the gently angled snow slope above. Under such circumstances, if we all remained tied to the rope, there was the danger that if one fell they would pull the other two off as well. If there was going to be an accident, we all reasoned that one death was better than three.

Already Mike and Nick had dropped behind and the entire group became more spread out as we climbed up the snow slope. Mark was setting a relentless pace. I tried to keep up with him, but also soon dropped behind. He was stronger, but I could not help feeling resentful of the fact that compared to Sean and me the load he was carrying was a smaller proportion of his body weight.

As the first light of dawn appeared, we caught Mark up waiting below where the ground steepened. A band of rock barred the way. It was going to be necessary to pitch the climbing. We emptied the ropes and climbing kit from our rucksacks and then I set off. The climbing, up ice-filled cracks between patches of snow, was difficult. It was tricky to find the best way within the limited scope of the head-torch beam and my hands got very cold when I had to remove my gloves to place pieces of equipment into the rock to safeguard my progress. By the time Mark and Sean joined me at the belay it was already light.

Sean led off above, as the chill went from the air. When we reached the next belay, both Mark and I were sweating heavily. It was nice to rest, to let my heavy breathing subside and to admire the views. We had cleared the rock band and snow slopes lay above again. It was hard to understand why it had taken so long to find a way through the ice-fall. It now looked obvious from above. Mike and Nick were just beginning the steeper section of climbing.

Suddenly, shouting shattered the silence,

'It's easy up here,' echoed around.

Then almost immediately I heard a familiar hissing sound and looked up to see one of the ropes being dropped down.

'What the hell's he playing at?' asked Sean.

'I don't know,' I replied, moments before the second rope followed.

'I guess we're climbing without ropes now,' Sean added sarcastically.

'That's all very well,' I hissed. 'But who's going to carry Mark's bloody rope?'

Mark was away now. I could see the outline of his arms and shoulders as he pounded his axes in before moving up the slope. We had divided the gear and food out equally before the climb and part of Mark's share had been one of the ropes he had dropped down. We would simply have to add the rope to everything else we were carrying.

We redistributed what we were carrying between us and set off. The sacks felt heavy, but got heavier still as it got warmer and we shed clothing. Then at about seven o'clock the sun hit and our progress slowed to a crawl, as snow on the slope turned to slush. I just wanted to get out of the sun and go to sleep. Mark had disappeared and there was nowhere to pitch a tent. We would have to carry on until we reached the ridge, where I suspected Mark was waiting for us. I quickly emptied my water bottle and my head began to throb. I dearly wanted to abandon my rucksack, but knew I would have to return for it. As time went by, I spent longer doing nothing, slumped over my axes. However I was not the only one suffering. I was slowly pulling away from Sean, and Mike and Nick were nowhere to be seen. It seemed ridiculous that a fine, sunny day that had passed without hitches was turning into such a struggle.

Finally the slope levelled out and I staggered along a shelf leading across to a notch in the ridge. Mark was lying on a foam mat in the snow, stripped to his vest.

'I've been here for two hours,' he bragged.

I could have been as well without carrying the rope, I thought. Mark's disregard for convention was in varying degrees exciting, funny and charming. Sometimes he went too far and could seem a little arrogant. But usually his attitude and behaviour meant he often ended up in strange situations doing unusual things and this generally made him great fun to be with. However, at times like these he was just plain annoying.

Without a word I threw my rucksack down and slumped on to it. The greatest concentration of high mountains in the world lay in front of me. To the east lay Mustagh Tower, K2, Broad Peak, the Gasherbrums and Chogolisa, clustered around the head of the Baltoro Glacier. If I looked in the other direction I could see the huge 1,500-metre face on the west side of the Greater Trango Tower – one of the world's largest vertical rock faces. The Nameless Tower stood nearby and another rock spire – Uli Biaho – in the valley behind. The climbing had required such effort that I had hardly noticed them.

I lay on the snow and marvelled at the view. Then, as Sean arrived, I took out my camera and framed a series of pictures. I knew the photographs would be stunning the moment I took them and felt privileged and humble to be in such a place. It was remarkable to think no others had viewed what we were looking at.

After a while we pitched the tent and dived inside in our underwear to escape the heat and sun. It was incredibly uncomfortable. We lay around and panted. Mark managed to get the stove going and make a brew. At midday Nick arrived.

'Mike's suffering with the heat and altitude,' he said. Mike was not having a very good time and I felt sorry for him, stuck down on the face in the searing glare of the sun. Nick rested while we made him a drink. Then he surprised us all by starting off down again. 'I'm going to help Mike,' he announced.

Four hours later Mike crawled into camp. Nick was carrying his rucksack. The day had been demanding enough inside our tent, and I could only imagine how much they had suffered. We helped them put up their tent nearby. Then, as the sun mercifully began to set, we tried to grab some sleep.

At midnight we were up again, collapsing the tent. By the time we had finished, my hands were cold. We moved off and climbed the gently angled snow ridge above. It was tiring work sinking into the deep, powdery snow and soon my feet were cold as well.

I was leading the steepest section of the ridge when the dawn began. As the horizon to the east gradually brightened I saw lightning flickering inside a mass of thunder heads. The sky above turned amazing shades of blues, violets and purples. Beams of light cut through the gaps in the cloud and illuminated distant mountains. Then suddenly the sun popped up from behind the West Ridge of K2, bathing the mountains all around in a rich, orange light. Tears poured from my eyes and rolled down my cheeks. I wiped them away with my hands and they froze to my gloves. I looked down at the others and watched their heads darting one way then the other, trying to take everything in.

The light show did not last long. The sun climbed quickly and we reached a notch on the ridge as it began to get hot again. Above was a steep rocky buttress, which barred the way to the summit perhaps four hundred metres above.

'We could go to the top from here,' Mark suggested as we dug out yet another platform for the tent.

'We'll wait and see what the weather does,' I cautioned.

I lay in the tent, hoping that the spell of clear skies that had blessed our time in the mountains would continue, but the signs did not look good. The wind increased and high clouds gathered. Then as the tent heated up, I developed a splitting headache. After suffering all day, I took some aspirins and the pain went away, making me feel very stupid for not taking some earlier. As the light faded, the sky cleared and I hoped we would get the extra decent day we needed in order to summit.

I awoke suddenly. The tent was shaking violently and snow was hissing in through the entrance which we had left slightly unzipped to allow some air to circulate. I sat up, leaned across Mark and Sean and closed the zip. It looked as if we would not get a chance to go to the summit on this occasion. As the weather deteriorated, the others woke up. By six in the morning, we were all sat with our backs up against the end of the tent, bracing it against the wind.

'Let's clear off,' Mark said, after a particularly severe gust, expressing what we had all been thinking for some time.

Outside, the driven snow stung our eyes. Visibility was less than ten metres and it was difficult to determine which was the slope below and which was sky. Our tracks from the previous day had all drifted over.

'Which way?' Mark yelled into my ear.

'This way,' I replied, striding off down the slope.

There was no way of knowing for certain if I was going in the right direction. It felt right, but without any way of checking all I could do was trust my senses. I ploughed on down, occasionally pausing to squint into the wind and snow to see if I could find the horizon, any feature that was recognisable. Nothing appeared, and as time went on I began to imagine that I had made some terrible mistake. The big worry was straying too far from the ridge. Then we would be left stranded on a large, open face of snow and ice above enormous cliffs. However, I did not want to get too close to the ridge either, as in sections standing waves of snow formed huge cornices, which we had been careful to avoid on the way up. With the present visibility it would be easy for us to wander on to one of these features and only realise the error as it collapsed beneath our feet. The lower we descended the more paranoid I became.

Then surprisingly the sky brightened, and looking up through the cloud I could just make out the outline of the sun. Way off to our right the rolling outline of the ridge slowly came into focus. A tiny, radiant splash of yellow marked the site of Mike and Nick's tent. Without pausing, I turned and made straight for it. Then the sky darkened and the tent and ridge were once more engulfed in cloud. It no longer mattered, my bearings were set. Ten minutes later we arrived at the camp.

'We're going down,' I shouted, shaking the tent.

There was some movement inside, before the entrance was unzipped and Nick's head appeared.

'We're going to sit it out,' he said, grimacing at the weather.

Being able to see the tent on the ridge had been a lucky break. It marked the point where we needed to descend straight down, to drop into the narrow ramp line that we had followed on the way up. We set off down without the intense, draining concentration of the first part of the descent. We no longer had to worry about getting lost.

After walking for a way, we down-climbed to the rock band. Three simple abseils brought us to the top of the slope that dropped on to the plateau. Mark was in a hurry to get off the mountain and galloped off down the snow slope, dragging Sean and me behind him with the rope. After the slow progress higher up it was exhilarating to be moving quickly again, and the deep, wet snow allowed us to stumble and slide without losing control. In a matter of minutes we had descended most of the slope and jumped the bergschrund.

We were some way short of the plateau when the snow finished and we walked on to ice. It was an extension of the main glacier running up the slope above. It was an unusual feature, which I would have expected to have been much steeper. I hardly gave it a second thought until Mark was about a hundred metres above the plateau. Suddenly he sat down and started bum-sliding. Moments later Sean was pulled from his feet by the rope. Already I could see they were sliding down the ice far too quickly for safety. A horrible fear welled up inside me. I took two large steps forward, and as the rope came taut sat down on the ice. I reasoned that it was better to slide on my backside, than to be pulled from my feet and possibly cartwheel. I lifted my feet to stop my crampons catching on the ice, then there was a sharp tug at my waist where the rope was tied to my harness and I was off.

The toboggan ride was short and brutal. I accelerated rapidly and a series of bone-jarring impacts passed through my backside and up my spine. I saw Mark and Sean spill out on to the snow at the base of the slope and for a moment thought I was going to escape unhurt. Then I bottomed out again. My vision blurred and I felt nauseous.

I came to a halt in the snow and lay groaning. Pain ran down my back and into my right leg. I could hear Mark laughing. Slowly my breathing calmed and I tried to sit upright. A surge of pain made me lie down again.

'Are you okay?' asked Sean, looking concerned.

'No,' I replied angrily, annoyed by the pointless nature of my injury. Now none of us would get off the mountain quickly.

With Sean's help I managed to get to my feet, but I was in so much pain that it was difficult to move.

'It's no good,' I said. 'I'll have to take a Temgesic.'

I found the packet of painkillers in my rucksack and slipped one under my tongue. A few minutes later, after the pill had dissolved I felt nauseous again. It did little to ease the pain.

There seemed little point in delaying what was going to be a long descent. I put my right arm around Sean's shoulders and we set off, trying to follow Mark's footprints. It was difficult because of the size of his stride and I often broke through into the soft, wet snow around his steps. As I sank up to my thighs, pain seared up my back. There was further agony as I struggled to extract myself.

Once we were off the plateau and we began to drop down

through the ice-fall, it was more comfortable for Sean simply to tow me through the snow. However there were crevasses to cross. The only way was to jump, which caused a massive surge of pain and left me gasping. As we dropped height, the snow turned to rain. By about midday we were off the snowy upper reaches of the glacier and conditions under foot improved. I was able to hobble slowly on the surface of the ice and rocks.

'I'll see you back at the camp,' Mark said, handing me his ski-poles before running off into the mist.

'You might as well leave me to it,' I told Sean after he had been watching my painfully slow steps for thirty minutes. There was little he could do to help me, and as my movements were slow and deliberate it seemed unlikely that I would injure myself further in a fall.

I staggered down the glacier feeling sorry for myself. It looked like this was the end of my expedition. I had obviously done some serious damage to my lower back or pelvis. The pain was just about bearable, but I had to stop frequently to let it subside. Climbing the loose scree slope above the glacier to reach the ridge of moraine which ran down to the camp was agony. The darkening cloud, mist and driving rain seemed to match my mood. I could hardly remember such a miserable afternoon.

When I finally arrived in camp, it was nearly dark. All I wanted to do was sleep, hoping that when I woke my injury would have somehow disappeared. I ate a little under the kitchen shelter, but it was not an evening for sitting around. The rain was still falling heavily and I was pleased we had taken the decision to come down, despite what had happened during our retreat. I joined Mark in the tent. By lying on my left side and packing clothing around my backside I finally made myself comfortable. I had no intention of moving until the morning.

I had barely fallen asleep when I woke to the tent shaking.

'Quick, much water coming,' Haqeem was shouting.

'Go and sleep with Sean,' I snapped, convinced that

his tent must have been leaking. 'We'll sort it out in the morning.'

'No. No. Much water coming soon.' There was panic in his voice.

'Shit,' Mark groaned. 'I'll go and see what he's going on about.'

He slid out of his sleeping bag, put on a waterproof jacket, grabbed his head-torch and putting his feet into his boots stepped outside. I could hear him and Haqeem running around, their voices sounded very serious.

'Get up now!' Mark burst into the entrance of the tent. 'There's a flood coming.'

I began to pull myself upright. The pain was intense, as the muscles around the injured area had stiffened while I was asleep. Now I could hear the water. It sounded like a torrent.

'Get a move on,' Mark shouted.

'Give me a hand then,' I demanded.

Mark dived into the tent and stuffed equipment into rucksacks while I tried to put on a few clothes. Then he leapt out again and pulled me out of the tent and stood me upright. Sean was also up. I helped as best as I could as Mark ripped the tent pegs from the ground. A wave of water washed round my ankles.

'Pick this up,' Mark screamed as the water hit the tent.

We grabbed each end and lifted the shelter above the encroaching flood. Suddenly it seemed everywhere was covered in water. As the water level rose above our boots, we ploughed uphill until finally Mark's head-torch beam picked out a raised dry spot next to Sean's tent. We made for it and dropped the tent down. The pain in my back returned and there was little I could do but stand and watch as the others tried to salvage the remaining tents and the kitchen.

Now I realised what had happened. After the prolonged rain, a river had started to flow along a narrow valley at the side of a moraine ridge which ran down into the camp. We were surrounded by a further moraine ridge and cliffs leaving nowhere for the water to escape. A lake had formed over the grassy meadow where we had pitched our tents.

After moving the kitchen the others returned, pitched my tent and insisted that I get some sleep. I was happy to oblige. I was beginning to think the day had no end. Finally, I rearranged my bedding and fell into a deep sleep.

In the morning the water had drained a little and I watched Mark, Sean and Haqeem building a dam to divert the main flow of water further down the valley. It was only partially successful, as sections kept breaking.

'Now I know what it was like to live in Holland in the eighteenth century,' Mark joked.

At midday, Mike and Nick returned. Mike had suffered severe headaches for two days before they had decided to come down. Their retreat had been both terrifying and arduous, as they descended avalanche-prone slopes and then waded through nearly metre-deep snow on the plateau.

It seemed that with the flood some of our momentum and enthusiasm were washed away, along with much of the kitchen. Mike decided he would limit his further activities to collecting rock samples in the valley. Mary Rose returned a day later from a trip to K2 Base Camp with the liaison officer and she chose to start making her way home to New Zealand.

My back gradually healed, marked by an enormous purple, red and yellow bruise running from my buttock down the back of my right leg. I teamed up with Nick and along with Mark and Sean we made two further attempts on the mountain, but luck was not with us. Each time we reached the ridge, bad weather set in, forcing us back down.

On a bright beautiful morning a group of porters arrived and we packed up the camp. We had arranged our collection date with them and there was no realistic way of changing it and besides, the food we had brought in with us was also coming to an end. The time to leave had arrived. We crossed the Baltoro Glacier to Urdukas where we joined the main trail to K2. Sean and I stayed behind for a while as the others followed the porters down. It was a beautiful place high on a terrace above the glacier, looking straight across to the mountains we had been among in the previous weeks.

It was a little frustrating not to climb to the summit of Biale, but the uncertainty of our undertaking had been the main attraction for me. However the excitement involved in attempting an unclimbed peak in such a remarkable place more than outweighed any disappointment I was feeling.

We had no intention of using the porters who had carried loads up to the base camp. After arriving we had been forced to take a visit to Urdukas to replace the flour and rice that had been taken during the walk-in. While we were there, we hired ten porters in advance for the walk-out. A week later two of the porters had arrived with fresh loads of flour and rice. The loads had been paid for in advance and so it was obvious the men were trustworthy. The men turned out to be of a completely different calibre to the ones who had carried for us on the way in. These porters were strong, fit and well organised. They simply wanted to get the job done as quickly and efficiently as possible. They had made five carries to K2 base camp already that summer. They told us they could complete the two week walk-up in eight days, and then ran down in three to obtain work with another expedition. For them, to get work on their way down was a bonus.

Walking down with our new employees was a pleasure. I warmed to the men immediately. They set off at a blistering pace and kept it up, although they did take regular breaks. At lunchtime they stopped and made tea on tiny fires of precious fire wood, carried up from Paiyu. We sat and shared thick, unleavened Balti bread and washed it down with the tea. Then one of the men marched off into a boulder field and returned clutching a bag. The bag was full of cigarettes. I laughed. As the only non-smoker in the group, he had stashed the cigarettes on the way up knowing the others would run out. Now he was selling them for a two rupee per packet profit.

When we reached Paiyu that evening I watched the men quietly organising themselves. Some made bread, while others collected wood. Then one man removed his boot to reveal a split a centimetre deep in the leathery skin of his heel. He pulled a strand of thread from one of the woven polypropylene bags in which we had packed the loads, threaded it through a rusty curved needle and sewed up the wound. These were hardy, honest people whom I felt the utmost respect for.

Despite being in such an alien environment and a long way from home, I felt content and relaxed. For me, it was starting to feel like my home.

Sean arrived late at the camp that night, having spent some time filming and taking photographs at Urdukas. He came straight over to where Mark and I were sitting. 'You're never going to guess what I saw after you left?' he said seriously.

'No idea,' I replied casually, not expecting anything important.

'Those ice-cliffs above the plateau on Biale fell down. They took out the whole fucking basin.'

We laughed nervously, quite aware of how many nights we had spent camped below the cliffs, but made light of Sean's news. It was back in Sheffield over a year later that Sean showed us some film footage he had been taking when the avalanche had occurred. We sat open-mouthed, watching the cloud of ice and snow engulfing the entire plateau and many hundreds of metres further down the valley. There was no doubt that such an event would have killed us had we been there at the time. The film was unedited and immediately after the pictures of the avalanche it cut to three choughs pecking at rubbish around the campsite at Urdukas. We all laughed at the coincidence and symbolism, imagining that we would have been reincarnated as the birds.

For me this was the first time that I realised the arbitrary and random nature of the risks I took going to climb in big mountains. It showed me it was possible to get killed even if you were careful, took the right decisions and did not make mistakes. In subsequent years, I have seen more outrageous and unpredictable events that had the potential to be fatal. In each case, as on Biale, I would never have thought they were possible. Yet this knowledge has never bothered me sufficiently to stop returning to those places. I have learned to accept this arbitrary risk and view it in a similar way to the risk I take every time I get into a car, although obviously I realise the risks associated with being in big mountains are much higher.

Chapter Five

Lost in Asia

'Wake up! Wake up!'

I opened my eyes and looked around the cramped, squalid hotel room. Sean was stirring on a bed nearby. The floor space was covered with our kit. A rusty old fan creaked slowly round on the ceiling above my head. I looked to my side – Mark's bed was empty. He was standing in the open door looking very worried.

'Have you seen my money belt?' he pleaded.

'Hardly,' I replied cynically. 'I've been asleep.'

'It was on my bed before I went for a shower.'

'Are you sure?' said Sean.

We quickly arose from our beds and joined Mark in a frantic search. I did not really share his concern, as he had been losing things and then finding them again for the entire length of the expedition. I became so annoyed with the habit while we were climbing that I lent him a lighter only whenever he needed to light the stove, and then demanded its return before he had time to lose it. I expected the money belt to drop from a rucksack, or be found among a pile of clothing. After we had searched everything several times I was not so sure. Sean checked the bathroom and came back into the room shaking his head.

'It's been nicked,' Mark said, slumping on to his bed and burying his face in the palms of his hands.

'What was in it?' Sean asked sympathetically.

'Fucking everything. Passport, air tickets, travellers' cheques, money. The lot.'

I let out a big sigh. It was every traveller's worst nightmare. We were due to catch a flight to Nepal in two days' time.

'How can it possibly have been stolen?' I pointed out.

'I left the door open while I was in the shower.'

Mark stormed out of the room and Sean shrugged at me as if to say, 'what did he expect?' On our way into the mountains Mike and Nick had refused to stay in the seedy hotel in the centre of Rawalpindi's sprawling Rajah Bazaar. Now their decision had been vindicated. We sat in silence as Mark stormed from one room to another, accusing other residents. Then he became involved in a blazing row with the manager. Eventually, he returned to the room.

'Lend me some money. I'm going to the police station.'

When Mark returned in the evening he looked ashen.

'You are not going to believe what happened to me.'

We listened while Mark told us his story. He had gone to the main police station in the city to report the theft, but because he was a foreigner he had been referred to the Deputy Police Commissioner. When Mark finally got to see the Commissioner, he was called out on a case and insisted that Mark accompany him. They drove in a police jeep through a labyrinth of back streets and eventually stopped at a small warehouse. Inside, a man was hanging by his neck from a piece of rope around a rafter.

Later, he learned that he could not get new travellers' cheques issued without a passport, and the airlines would not issue replacement tickets. The British Embassy could only give him documents to travel back to Britain. Mark had not had a good day.

In the morning we packed and prepared to leave. The three of us had all been invited to join a further expedition in Nepal before we had left home. Now Sean and I needed to catch a train to Karachi, if we were going to make our flight to Kathmandu. There was nothing more we could do to help Mark. We gave him enough money to tide him over for a few days and then engaged in an uneasy bout of hand shaking and back slapping. It was difficult to know what to say.

'See you in Nepal and if not, back in Sheffield,' I said with an optimism I did not feel. I felt sure Mark was on his way home. It was a sad way to part.

We stepped out of the bus and walked across the car park towards the airport terminal building.

'We'd better get on this flight today,' Sean grumbled.

We had turned up the day before and discovered that our flight to Kathmandu had been overbooked. Despite having tickets, as late arrivals at the check-in we had lost our seats. However, we had been put up in a hotel overnight and promised a place on the next plane. We would soon find out if the promise was good.

'Hey look! There's Mark,' Sean exclaimed as we approached the steps leading into the departure hall.

'Are you sure?' I asked, but I had already seen his unmistakable frame.

'Mark!' Sean yelled, and he turned towards us.

We started laughing simultaneously. Mark was wearing a ridiculous pair of tiny half sunglasses, that did little to hide a pair of black eyes. The rest of his face was grossly swollen and bruised.

'What happened to you?' we chorused, even though it was obvious he had been in a fight.

Mark said nothing and was deeply uncomfortable with our presence. His embarrassment only fuelled our laughter and further questioning. It took us two days of persistent inquiry to extract and piece together the whole story.

After we had left Rawalpindi, Mark had his first stroke of good luck for days – his passport was handed in at the British Embassy. Then, with a little more good fortune, he had run into a friend, Jon Tinker, in the street. Jon had kindly lent

Mark enough money to buy a new air ticket to Kathmandu. To make up time he bought an extra flight from Islamabad to Karachi. Everything was organised in a great hurry. Finally, he packed and dived into a taxi asking to be taken to the airport. Unfortunately, Mark did not have enough money left for the fare. When they reached the airport, he slapped his remaining change into the driver's hand and jumped from the taxi. The driver followed, grabbed him and demanded the rest of his money. A heated argument developed. The intense stress and frustration Mark had been feeling for the previous few days soon spilled over into violence and he ended their disagreement with a single punch. If the event had occurred on the street Mark's size would have probably deterred others from getting involved, but the other drivers at the taxi-rank took a dim view of his actions against a fellow worker. The men soon organised themselves and rushed him. By the time the frenzied mob had finished, Mark had received a severe beating.

Staring out of the window of the plane, I marvelled at the radiant landscape below. After weeks in the brown, barren, dusty wilderness of the Pakistani Karakoram, flying over the lush foothills of Eastern Nepal was very pleasing to the eyes. The early morning sun reflected from the patchwork of tiny, terraced paddy fields filled by the monsoon rains. Clumps of pretty little village houses flashed by and occasionally the cultivated land gave way to sections of jungle and forest criss-crossed with prominent ridge-top tracks. As the plane flew further into the mountains, pine trees and Rhododendrons clung to the higher hillsides.

It had been Mark who suggested I telephone Doug Scott and ask to join an expedition to Makalu – the world's fifth highest mountain. I could hardly believe it when he had said, 'Aye kid, come along.' To me it was an honour to be asked to go on a trip with someone of Doug's stature in the mountaineering world. This was a man I had been reading about in books for years, who had climbed Everest's

South West Face and crawled down the Ogre. Now, as the plane wound its way up the valleys of eastern Nepal, the reality of where I was and what I was doing still had a dream-like quality.

After forty minutes of flying, the plane narrowly cleared a ridge top and began to drop into a deep-sided valley. The pilot levelled out about 500 metres above the river and followed its track. Suddenly we rounded a corner, and there on a terrace above a bend in the river lay the airfield of Tumlingtar. I barely had time to register the fact, before the plane plunged nose first towards the tiny strip of grass. I watched the ground come up to meet us through the cockpit windows of the small twin-propeller aircraft. Just as we were about to smash into the hillside before the runway, the pilot skilfully trimmed the aircraft, lifted the nose and we hit the grass with a loud thud. Then he wrestled with the controls as the machine aqua-planed through water lying on the field. We slid one way, then another, eventually skidding to a halt just metres from a fence marking the end of the runway. I slowly released my hands from the armrests of my seat and let out a loud sigh. Moments later the door opened and we were allowed to leave the plane. The steamy heat hit me instantly. Here at the bottom of this river valley we were lower than in Kathmandu, and as if to emphasise the point bananas grew around the airport perimeter.

I had flown in with Greg Child, an Australian-born American resident, who also had a big name in the climbing world. The other team members, who had left Kathmandu a few days earlier to walk from a roadhead, were, we were told, in a small town just up the trail. After a cup of tea we began to walk.

The first hill gave a taste of things to come. The horrendous humidity soon had us stripped to our shorts, trying desperately to remain in the tiny pool of shade provided by our umbrellas. The strength seemed to ebb from my body along with my sweat. Then clouds filled the hazy sky and it began to rain. This gave some relief from the heat, but turned the surface of the track into red mud. We slipped regularly and on the steepest sections of path it was difficult to remain upright for long.

In order to make the most of the post-monsoon climbing season, we had started walking into the mountains while the rains were still in progress, hoping to be ready to begin climbing as soon as they finished. Over the ten days it took to walk to the base camp, I quickly realised why most tourists avoid the entire country of Nepal, and trekking there in particular, during the monsoon season.

We toiled first through paddy fields and leech infested jungle, then dripping forests of rhododendron and finally sodden grassy hillsides. It rained every day.

On the second night, an earthquake registering 6.7 on the Richter Scale shook us awake just before dawn. For a few seconds we bounced on the ground in our ridge-top camp, listening to the sound of pots falling over in the kitchen tent and landslides crashing down nearby hillsides. Then the tremors stopped. We had been lucky: four people died in the closest town, Khanbari, and later we learned that hundreds had been killed on the plains of Nepal and Northern India to the south.

While we remained in the lower foothills, the leeches were a constant annoyance. They swayed on vegetation at the side of the path, somehow tracking your progress as you passed. If you did stop they homed in on you, propelling themselves by a strange end-to-end movement reminiscent of a Slinky spring. If bare flesh was showing, they could attach themselves immediately, injecting both an anaesthetic to suppress pain and an anti-coagulant to prevent blood clotting. Otherwise, they could squeeze themselves through tiny holes in clothing before feeding. Once gorged with blood they dropped off leaving a pain-free wound which could bleed for hours and then develop into a tropical ulcer in the following days. On many evenings I removed my walking boots to find my socks drenched with blood. Sometimes we were lucky enough to catch them feeding. Pulling them off was the most messy form of removal, but a dab with a lighted cigarette made them drop to the ground squirming. Later, we all took to carrying film canisters filled with salt to shake on to leeches, which squirmed, shrivelled, and then burst once it was administered. 'Death by osmosis,' Mark called it.

Doug had arranged for a fee-paying group of trekkers to accompany us to the base camp to help cover the expedition's costs. I felt sorry for them. Normally trekking groups operate in Nepal during the much drier pre- and post-monsoon periods, when they can expect fine settled weather and superb views of the mountains. Here they had to suffer the heat, rain and an earthquake, without any of the stunning views they could have expected to see at other times. The group had found the leeches particularly unpleasant. One man had been so bothered by them that he took to wearing a full set of waterproofs inside his sleeping bag. One night he woke up screaming with a leech attached to his nose – the only exposed part of his body.

However, the worst part of the entire walk was near the end, after we had left the relative comfort of the last village. Crossing the Shipton La – a 5,100-metre high pass named after the British mountaineer and explorer who was the first westerner to cross, it rained torrentially for three days without a break. Eventually, paths became rivers and even the surface of the ground ran with water. As we walked higher, the temperature dropped, everybody and everything became utterly drenched and both expeditioners and locals alike developed stinking colds. Our porters hired in the lowlands deserted us, leaving their loads scattered up the hillside. In the confusion most of our food went missing.

It was a relief to finally drop down from the pass in improving weather into the Upper Barun Valley. It was impossible to imagine a more wild, remote and beautiful place, where feathery lichen metres in length hung from the trees. There we met a family of yak herders living in squalid conditions under a boulder. Only a small area of their living space was dry. The woman of the family pleaded with us to help. Her husband lay semi-conscious on the ground, poisoned by toxins from an enormous abscess on his thigh. His father lay dead under a blanket at the back of the shelter. The beautiful valley was also a prison, as the family had been unable to escape over the pass in such appalling weather conditions with two very ill members. Fortunately, one of our expedition doctors – Brian McGowan – operated on the man, lancing his abscess with a Swiss Army Knife and cleaning the wound before providing him with a course of life-saving antibiotics.

Finally, we made it to base camp, only for many of the expedition members to contract flu. Then a tragedy struck. A cook-boy died in the night from pulmonary oedema – an altitude-related illness, when the lungs fill with fluid – despite the tireless efforts of our two doctors to save him.

A few days later we moved the base camp higher and most expedition members elected to stay at the higher camp. Feeling ill, I descended and lay immobilised in my tent for four days. I thought I might have flu, but there were some unusual symptoms. Eventually, I felt a little better and longed for some company after the days spent with two Nepali cooks who had a very limited knowledge of English. I also wanted to consult the doctors about my illness. Leaving the camp early in the morning, I made a concerted effort to reach the higher camp. The way up the Barun Glacier was long and tiring. I had to stop frequently for rests and as the day went on the rests became longer. When the late afternoon cloud descended and the temperature dropped, I began to get worried. Climbing up a boulder field above the glacier was a desperate struggle. I found myself literally crawling the last few hundred metres into the camp.

I made my way into the mess tent, feeling completely exhausted. The two expedition doctors pointed at me and started laughing, quickly followed by the others in the shelter. I felt a little hurt. It was not the welcome I had hoped for during my struggle to reach the camp.

'You've got hepatitis!' they shouted in unison. Having not

had a mirror in the lower camp I had been unable to see how yellow my face had become.

For me the expedition was as good as over. It had been a disaster from beginning to end. I did wonder for a while where I had picked up the illness, but since I had not been exactly careful about what I drank and ate it was impossible to tell. In Pakistan, Mark and I had formed an exclusive organisation called 'The Dangerous Eating Club'. We were the club's only two members. We took turns at picking the filthiest street stalls to eat from. It was a rather reckless game of dare. We had been no more careful since arriving in Nepal. Another reason tourists avoided the country in the monsoon was because of disease. As the rains fell, drains backed up and sewage and drinking water mixed. The incidence of water-borne diseases increased dramatically. As we never treated water, whatever the source, I could have picked the illness up virtually anywhere.

'You don't look after yourself very well kid,' Doug commented perceptively.

Looking back now I can see I was a little reckless, but it was all part of a philosophy that involved engaging with people whatever their culture, social class or status and seeing what developed. Sometimes things went wrong and I ended up in places and situations that I would rather have avoided, but mostly this approach brought illuminating experiences. To me it seemed a shame to visit such places and to exclude or dismiss experiences simply because somewhere looked dirty and the inhabitants poor. Besides, with very limited funds my money went further if I lived cheaply. On this occasion I had miscalculated. For the want of a small bottle of tincture of iodine to treat water, I had got ill.

I stayed a few days at the upper camp, feeling very sick and too weak to consider what my next move would be. My disease was very colourful. In addition to the yellow skin, I passed china clay stools and pissed best bitter. The others were not particularly sympathetic. The doctors worried about the danger of infection and insisted that I use my own set of eating utensils. A skull and cross bones was drawn with a marker pen on to a plate and cup, and I carried around my own spoon and fork.

Drained of my usual energy I initially felt depressed, and as the others moved up towards higher camps, the realisation of what I had lost began to sink in. I would not get a chance to climb with top-grade climbers such as Doug Scott and Greg Child. Not only had I missed the opportunity to climb Makalu, but I would not get the chance to learn from two such experienced mountaineers.

Yet as one opportunity was denied to me, I could see others opening up. I had scraped together a small amount of savings before leaving home, with the intention of travelling on through Asia to Australia, where my brother had been living for the previous two years. I was looking forward to seeing him again and spending some time with him. I would also be able use his house as a base while I worked and saved some money, before going on a rock climbing tour of Australia.

Earlier in the year I had met a bubbly and enthusiastic woman in the King's House Hotel in Glencoe. We got on instantly and spent the evening talking at the bar. Anne Murray was intelligent, pretty and heavily involved in outdoor sports. She was great fun to be with. For many years I had never made much effort when it came to getting girlfriends, perhaps because I was so preoccupied with climbing and forever on the move. At parties and other social gatherings, I often found myself talking to other male climbers rather than to the women who were gathered there. Not surprisingly, my relationships were infrequent and usually brief. By coincidence Anne and I met several times over the following month, both in Scotland and Leeds, where she was in her last year at college. A wonderful day's climbing on Minus Two Gully on Ben Nevis's North Face seemed to cement our relationship. As winter turned into spring we started to see each other on a regular basis and by the time I was ready to leave for Pakistan we had agreed to meet in Kathmandu and share the journey to Australia together.

Now my climbing had ended early I would be able to get back to Kathmandu, to meet up with Anne and to start my travels earlier than I had planned.

I looked around the cramped hotel room and then at my watch. We had three hours to sort out all the clothing, food and kit that was lying over the beds and floor. We needed to decide what to take and what to leave behind, then we would have to pack and take the half-hour journey by taxi to the airport. There was barely enough time and Anne had not returned from her shopping trip yet. I could not understand why she was not back, but I concentrated on sorting out my own belongings.

I heard some arguing beneath the room in the hotel foyer, but thought little about it until I realised Anne was involved. The argument seem to spill up the stairs and then stopped suddenly. Seconds later Anne burst into the room. She was very upset and looked as if she had been crying.

'What's the matter?' I demanded.

'You're not going to believe this Si,' Anne replied with a touch of hysteria. 'My locked bike was stolen. I went back to tell them in the hire shop and they demanded the money to replace it. I refused. Then they would not let me leave. They even threatened and hit me. That's why I am so late.'

'Let's go and sort this out,' I said, heading for the door.

I rushed downstairs with Anne following me, and confronted the man who was now engaged in a heated debate in Nepali with the hotel owner. I wanted to know why he had hit Anne. He wanted 1,500 rupees to replace the stolen cycle. He was not going to apologise. I was not going to give him any money. Time slowed. The hotel manager tried to act as an intermediary, but to me he seemed to be siding with the cycle-hire man. I was incensed that neither seemed to see anything wrong in hitting Anne. I stormed back upstairs.

'I know it's going to end in a fight,' I heard Anne say.

Then, without really knowing how or why, I was back in the foyer arguing with the man again. I was up close, yelling at him now. He tried to push me away and I bundled him out of the door into a small courtyard. Then I watched my right arm take a massive swing, before landing a powerful punch on his forehead. He staggered backwards looking more dazed and surprised than hurt, as I picked up a plant pot. Perhaps it was Anne's screaming or maybe the arrival of some of his friends that prevented me from smashing it on his head. Whatever the cause, I noticed myself clutching a plant pot, shaking with rage with lots of people staring at me. The man I had hit now seemed to have fully recovered from my blow. I suddenly felt rather stupid. I put the pot down and calmly walked back inside and up to our room. As I began packing again I noticed the pain in my right hand. It was already quite swollen. The pain seem concentrated around the knuckle of my index finger. I sat down on a bed and took some deep breaths. I had almost felt like a spectator for the whole fight.

'I'm going to pay him,' Anne announced coming back into the room. She picked up her money belt and went downstairs.

It was only then that I noticed Anne's sister Helen. She had quietly watched the whole drama unfold from the room. I had only met her in Kathmandu two weeks earlier. She looked completely shocked. What must she be making of her sister's boyfriend?

Anne returned, I bandaged my hand and we resumed our packing.

'What about your hand, Si?' Anne asked once the bags were finished.

'Oh, don't worry about that. It'll be all right,' I replied, conscious of the fact that we had been preparing for our trek to Kanchenjunga for much of our stay in Kathmandu. Besides, I was now heartily sick of the city.

We took a taxi to the airport, arriving just in time to check in, and boarded the plane to Tumlingtar fifteen minutes later.

'I'm glad you hit him,' Anne said sympathetically once we were in the air.

As I gazed out of the windows down at the Nepalese foothills and the patchwork of terraced fields and felt the sharp pain in my hand, I was not so sure. There was none of the feeling of awe and excitement I usually associated with such moments. I felt drained and slightly depressed. For the first time since the fight I wondered exactly what damage I had done to myself. If I tried to clench my fist, the pain was very severe.

I felt better as soon as we landed at Tumlingtar. I was back among friends, back in the hills with the simple, trustworthy people that lived there. I hired a porter called Pasang to carry a single rucksack containing the stove, tent and food that we would need once we climbed up out of habitation and into the mountains. Then we began to walk.

'I don't believe where I am,' said Helen, staring at the old Nepali woman tending a copper pan of rice above a clay hearth in the centre of the small room.

We were three days into our trek to Kanchenjunga. I had wanted to visit the area because the Nepalese government had only recently opened it to independent trekkers. There had been no time for the Nepalese to develop any network of guest houses that line the trails of the more popular treks. Towards the end of each day we simply found whatever food and shelter was available for the night. Three wonderful days of trekking had passed, but for the first two nights we had stayed in villages that had basic hotels for passing locals. The tiny settlement of Hellok consisted of only about a dozen houses. As darkness fell, we had simply knocked on a door and agreed a price to stay the night with the old woman inside.

'I told you we'd only stay in the smartest places,' I replied jokingly.

Helen had spent the previous two years teaching English in Japan and had arranged to travel with Anne before returning to England to look for work. She was finding rural Nepal quite a contrast to Japanese cities and was not used to roughing it.

In the morning we were away early and left the main river

valley to follow a tributary that led up to the south side of Kanchenjunga. My cheap Nepali map showed the trail following the river. However, I soon began to have doubts as it was difficult to follow an indeterminate path up through the fields above the village. It became even trickier when we left the cultivated area and entered a partially cleared forest. Soon I ran up against a wall of jungle forcing me to walk along boulders at the side of the river. Finally, I stopped completely at a steepening of the river gorge, where a landslide barred the way, and waited for the others.

The sensible thing was to turn around, walk back to the village and to ask for directions, but to me there was something compelling about the way ahead. The terrain was interesting and would offer a challenge. 'Maybe there's a better path up ahead,' I offered when the others arrived.

We began to cross the landslide. Up higher, the river formed a gorge and we needed to be above it, so I contoured slightly up across the slope of dirt and gravel. The surface was quite slippy, but by kicking steps you could maintain balance. Soon we were high above the river. Helen began to get scared and twice I went back to help her. We went into the forest briefly before another slide blocked the way. I seriously considered going down.

Then surprisingly, a local appeared on the other side of the slide and waved at us. The man had a dramatic effect on Pasang, who dashed on ahead. I followed behind. The man kept waving enthusiastically and as we got closer to him I could see he was bare-footed and smiling. He was wearing just a pair of khaki shorts and a torn shirt, with a Kukri knife tucked into his belt. Both his clothes and his body were very dirty. He looked like he had been living in the forest for years. Then suddenly I looked up and the man had gone, as if he had melted into the jungle from which he had first appeared.

As we entered the canopy of the forest, Pasang started to come into his element. He was obviously very comfortable with this kind of terrain and I began to realise he was following a faint trail. Perhaps the jungle man we had seen earlier had been this way: occasionally there were little marks chopped on to the trunks of trees and bushes.

When the undergrowth was particularly dense, whoever had passed through the forest had cleared more defined paths. But the going was incredibly slow. We started meeting cliffs barring the way. Some we could skirt round, but others had to be climbed, up vegetation-lined ramps and gullies. Helen was scared and I had to hold her hands and feet sometimes as we swarmed up and down vines and tree roots. At times I felt as if I was playing the lead role in a Tarzan movie.

I knew we were off the main trail, in effect lost, but I also knew that further up the valley we would meet a path again. We had to, as the valley we were following was formed by the Simbuwa Khola River which drained the whole of the south side of Kanchenjunga. The main path to the southern base camp had to enter the valley at some point. It was just a matter of time.

'Well, this is certainly an adventure,' I said glibly as we bedded down in our sleeping bags on the forest floor that night. The reply was a tense silence. There had not even been enough space to pitch the tent.

In the middle of the night, I awoke feeling uncomfortable and found lumps on my body. My head torch revealed that ticks had penetrated both my sleeping bag and my skin. I panicked.

'Anne. Wake up. Wake up.' I showed her the ticks. 'Please help me get them off.'

Anne removed two of the annoying insects from my body and one from my leg. They had already buried themselves into my skin. A tropical ulcer had also developed on my shin from an infected leech bite. I did not sleep well. Now the forest was beginning to make me edgy too.

In the morning we entered a zone of bamboo. If the undergrowth and cliffs had proved difficult to negotiate, this was worse. Before we could move forward it was necessary to pull the canes apart to create enough space to step into.

We made tortuously slow progress as the hours passed, but eventually the bamboo thinned and we entered more temperate forest, with pine trees and sparser undergrowth. I felt an immediate sense of relief. However, the undergrowth soon thickened again, slowing progress, until we had to return to climbing. By scrambling up and down banks we could follow the riverbed wherever possible, but the climbing was more exposed and difficult than it had been lower down.

'I'm worried about Helen, Si,' Anne confided in me as we set up the tent for the second night on a terrace next to the river. 'I'm okay, but it's tough for her. What happens if she has an accident?'

'Oh, she'll be all right,' I said with a confidence I did not feel.

To me, most of the time in the forest had been an adventure. It had livened up what would otherwise have been a pleasant but unchallenging walk. However, I had applied my own standards to everyone else. What was a challenge to me was outright dangerous to Helen – someone who had never even trekked before. I began to feel a responsibility for Helen that I should have felt right from the beginning of the walk. With that responsibility fixed in my mind, I soon realised the seriousness of our position. We were walking through uncharted terrain, with a rapidly diminishing food supply and only vague ideas about the direction to go and the distances involved. Now we had walked up for so long, the thought of going back down through the jungle was too hard to bear. We were committed. Walking on until we reached the path was likely to be much simpler than turning back. We would have to hold our nerve and carry on.

As we began our third day in the forest, I had a feeling of dread. We plodded along the riverbed wearily for a few minutes expecting a day like the previous two. Then, to our surprise, we climbed up on to the bank again and almost immediately we hit the main trail. I felt the burden of guilt and the nagging doubts that had begun to cloud my decisions lift instantly. I had been right to follow my gut instinct and feelings and stick with the course of action, even when it had proved difficult and dangerous.

A little later we sat in a clearing in the sun, eating strips of yak cheese, bought from a family of Sherpas living in a small hut. We were back in civilisation. As we walked further up the valley the trees thinned and snow-capped mountains appeared. Here was the remote mountain valley that I had almost begun to doubt existed.

That night we camped high in the mountains and left at first light to walk up to the base camp. It was a clear, crisp winter's day and the peaks of Jannu and Kanchenjunga stood at the head of a wonderful cirque of mountains.

High on a moraine ridge below the towering South Face of Kanchenjunga, which soared up to the complex summit of the world's third highest mountain, we met a German trekker, who invited us to dinner that evening. The offer was welcome as the extra time in the forest had seriously depleted our food supplies.

It turned out that Wolfgang was a doctor and he insisted on examining my bandaged hand.

'I think your hand is broken,' he said. 'You must get it treated.'

Perhaps it was because his was an outsider's opinion that the seriousness of the damage to my hand began to sink in. If I had thought about my injury rationally I would have come to the same conclusion much earlier. Instead I had chosen to ignore it, because I did not want it to interfere with my plans. 'I'm going to have to go back to Kathmandu and get my hand looked at,' I told Anne.

'Wolfgang has asked us trek with him for the next few days. Do you mind?' Anne asked a little later.

'You might as well.'

We walked south and climbed out of the valley that seemed to have held us captive for the previous few days. It was good to follow the path we should have used to enter the valley and to walk through the dense forest and jungle rather than actually inside it. We spent a further day walking together and then, in the beautiful little village of Yapudin, we said our goodbyes. I was sad to be leaving them. I was not looking forward to returning to Kathmandu, but also knew that if I delayed getting treatment for my hand much longer it might give me more serious long-term problems.

In two days I raced down through the foothills of Eastern Nepal to reach a roadhead at Phidim. It took two full days of local bus travel to wind down through the picturesque tea plantations around Ilam to reach the Terai in the far south-eastern corner of the country, and then on to Kathmandu. My backside was very sore when I finally arrived back in the city.

'Go to the Canadian Clinic,' someone suggested when I asked about my hand. 'They will sort out the best treatment for you.'

A Canadian doctor pivoted my index finger and, having watched the bone behind the knuckle protrude up into the skin, pronounced it broken.

'Better go and get some X-rays,' he said, giving me the address of a large local hospital elsewhere in the city.

I took a rickshaw to the hospital and was directed to the X-ray department, who sent me to the cashier to pay for them. Then I took the chit back to the X-ray department, who took some pictures. Some time later I was sent to another office to pick up the processed pictures. Back at the Canadian Clinic they looked at the transparencies, confirmed my hand was broken and gave me the address of an orthopaedic surgeon. Eventually, I found his tiny private clinic and was seen immediately, ahead of dozens of waiting patients. He wanted more X-rays and sent me with a letter to a corrugated iron shed down the road. To my amazement there was an X-ray machine inside.

'Now we need plaster,' announced the doctor, after studying the latest set of images.

'I'll just go and get some, shall I?' I offered. I was beginning to get the hang of this do-it-yourself medicine.

Armed with another letter I found a pharmacy close by and

bought the plaster. Finally, the doctor set the bone and I left. It had been an entertaining day and had only cost 20 dollars, including the rickshaw fares.

By the time Anne and Helen returned to Kathmandu my Nepalese visa had nearly expired. We agreed a place to meet in Goa and I left the next day for India.

I crossed the border in the night and caught a bus to Patna. My first views of India – a country I have since visited on numerous occasions – were of paddy fields gold in the early morning light and dotted with squatting Indians. A small water jug sat in the earth next to each figure, ready to be used to wash with once they had finished.

The pot on my own arm acted as a magnet. Whenever I walked down the street people's eyes lit up when they saw the lump of plaster on my forearm. It was every Indian's introduction to me. Often they would alter the direction they were walking in or cross the road to speak.

'What happened?' they would ask.

The perpetual questioning soon became annoying. After only two of the four weeks recommended for my arm to be in plaster, I snapped and took a penknife to the object of so much attention. Without the plaster I was much less conspicuous and at least when people did talk to me they used a different line of questioning.

My travels took me first to Calcutta and then on to Bombay, before I made my way to Goa. After finding a cheap room to rent in a family house, I settled nicely into beach life. For nearly a month through December the days passed in a lazy routine, which Anne and Helen's arrival did little to disrupt. A leisurely breakfast was usually followed by walking along the beach and some swimming, before finally visiting a restaurant and saluting the sun with a beer as it dipped below the horizon of the Indian Ocean.

At the end of December we finally motivated ourselves to do some more travelling. Helen set off with an ambitious schedule to tour southern India, while Anne and I opted to visit a place inland called Hampi, where we might be able to go rock climbing. We would meet up again in Calcutta, before our flights to Thailand.

On the way to Hampi we stopped at a place called Castle Rock, hoping to find the rock itself. In dense jungle Anne and I climbed while a troop of Hanuman monkeys swung through the trees all around. Later, while we were walking back to our lodgings along a railway track, a steam train passed by.

'I wish I could ride on one of those,' Anne said wistfully.

The following morning, on New Year's Day, a train sporting two banana palms and rows of bunting appeared as we walked back down the tracks for another day's climbing. As the train approached, I stuck my thumb out. The drivers leaned out and waved to us and then, to our amazement, stopped and we jumped on. For a few minutes we shovelled coal into the boiler and looked out of the porthole-like windows at the track ahead before they slowed to a stop and dropped us off.

When we reached the village of Hampi, it was immediately obvious that the place was going to exceed even our wildest expectations. Stepping off the bus in the main bazaar, we stood staring at the tall pyramid of the Virupaksha Temple, which was set in the middle of a ruined city and towered over the village. The landscape was equally striking. Between flat, fertile patches of banana plantations were hills covered in huge granite boulders. The ruins of temples, palaces, houses and huge city walls sat among the strange, almost surreal landscape. Troupes of monkeys moved nimbly through both boulders and buildings. An unhappy elephant lived chained to one of the pillars inside the temple. It vented its anger by swiping at people with pieces of sugar cane on which it was fed held in its trunk.

Our time in the place was simply magical. Sometimes we climbed on the largest and most attractive-looking boulders, but mostly we simply wandered around, exploring and marvelling at the beauty of both the land and the buildings and how each complemented the other so well. Every corner we turned offered another stunning view and a whole new set of climbs and ruins to discover, and it seemed that even as we got to know the area, we found something new with each fresh viewing.

Yet despite the physical beauty of Hampi, what made it really special were the feelings it evoked. When, during early evenings, we sat on one of the many hills watching the sun set, I felt the place had an undefinable, somehow spiritual quality. The only other times I have felt that way have been in particularly impressive mountains, or when some momentous event has occurred when I have been climbing in them.

All too quickly the days passed and we soon found ourselves making the long journey to Calcutta to meet up with Helen, before flying to Thailand.

Our time in India had been like a dream, whether it was spent walking around palaces and temples and the packed pavements of Calcutta or swimming off white sandy beaches of Goa at night with phosphorescent algae sparkling in the water. I felt that if you wanted something to happen strongly enough then in India it would. Anything was possible.

I was not prepared for the bustle, noise and pollution of downtown Bangkok, nor the wholesale western consumerism. Coming from India there seemed nothing even vaguely spiritual or mystical about Thailand. It was a culture shock from which I never really recovered.

Anne had a dream of buying a motorbike and travelling on it, and so we left Bangkok hoping to pick one up in the north-east of the country, leaving Helen to plan her own travel plans for the following month. It was good simply to escape the city. Rural Thailand was much more to my liking. At Nong Khai, on the banks of the Mekong River, Anne found someone interested in selling a bike and completed the purchase by filling in a set of illegible Thai ownership documents. She was now the proud owner of a small 125cc Honda motorcycle.

I was surprised when I actually managed to ride it down the main street and back again without either stalling or falling off. Growing up in the countryside, I had had many opportunities to ride motorbikes as a child and teenager, but I had never really taken to them. People would always encourage me to have a go, only to regret their suggestion as I took a tumble and damaged their prized machines. It had been many years since I had last ridden one for myself, although I often rode pillion on other people's bikes. Anne knew even less than I did. She had never ridden a motorbike before. So it was going to be a steep learning curve for both of us.

We bought a Thai road map and set off the next day, with a loose plan to follow Thailand's northern border. Once we were out of the town, I passed on my own limited knowledge with a half-hour riding lesson. Anne learnt quickly and we were soon able to ride the bike with similar levels of incompetence.

On our second day of riding, the rear tyre blew out on a straight section of road when we were travelling at some speed. The bike veered one way and then the other, and felt as though it was going to slide from under us. I grabbed hold of the handlebars from behind Anne and somehow we both managed to keep the bike upright.

It soon became apparent that the road map we had bought was very optimistic. In reality, many of the roads marked on the map either did not exist or were of a much lower grade than shown. We soon found ourselves riding along dirt tracks through dense, hilly jungle along the border with Laos. On a ridge top overlooking a river that formed the border, we came upon an army check post. The soldier manning the barrier looked very surprised to see us. We waited while he made a radio call. Then he checked our passports before lifting the barrier. I could hardly believe what lay a little further along the road. A large unit of soldiers in full combat gear were dug into an elaborate system of trenches on the hillside below the road. There were also a number of large gun emplacements, covered in camouflage webbing. It seemed we were in the middle of a war zone. We waved at the soldiers as we rode past, who looked completely bewildered to see us in such a place.

Slowly we progressed around the border, but there was a certain inevitability about the outcome. I felt that if we had continued to get up in the morning and ride 60 kilometres each day then eventually we would traverse Thailand's northern borders as we had set out to do. When I thought of what we were doing in those terms, I knew I could not get the same feeling of satisfaction as I would have at the successful conclusion of a mountaineering expedition.

The daily routine of it all started to bore me. We jumped from one tourist lodge to another, where we met other travellers, herded to the same places by the same guide book, who talked endlessly about the same things. Even the landscape changed little.

'Where did you stay in Chiang Rai? How much was it? Where is a good restaurant? How much is a meal?' they would ask.

Near the border of Burma we ended up following some very steep tracks through the jungle. Sometimes it was so steep that Anne got off and walked while I ran at particularly nasty sections. I fell off several times. Later, we ended up in a very remote village where the people were not happy to see us. We left amid a feeling of tension and I could only conclude that they did not appreciate our visit as they were probably involved in heroin production.

One day, while following the border further south, we came down a hill to be greeted by a crew at the bottom repairing the road. I was sitting on the back at the time and so could not work out fully what had happened, but we left the tarmac and entered the rutted, gravelly section of road works travelling far too quickly. As we began to climb uphill out of the hollow, the bike went from under us. Anne was propelled forward and clear of the machine, but somehow I remained attached to it. When we finally slid to a halt there was a searing pain coming from my left foot. Somehow it had got caught between the wheel and back mudguard as I had fallen. The rear suspension was now crushing my foot. 'Get it off! Get it off!' I shouted, frantically slapping the mudguard.

Anne, who seemed to have escaped the fall unharmed, took one look at my trapped foot and burst into tears, while the Thai road crew soon came running and then stood watching my writhing looking rather puzzled. Summoning all my strength and with a healthy amount of adrenalin flowing in my blood, I managed to pull the mudguard away from the wheel and free my foot. As soon as I did so the pain was even more intense. I angrily cursed at the men and hobbled off up the road, determined I was not going to give them the pleasure of watching me in agony.

We made it to the next town, but my foot swelled up like a melon and it was two days before I could travel again. I became convinced that our quest was going to end in tragedy and told Anne my fears.

'I think you're paranoid,' she told me.

I knew I was paranoid, but after the previous few months of what seemed like an endless stream of disease and injury, perhaps my attitude was not surprising. I had reached a point where I was actually prepared to change my behaviour to avoid any further distress.

My fear eventually reached such heights that I refused to ride the bike any more. We left it in a small town north of Bangkok and caught a coach back into the city, where we met up with Helen, who had been having a much more enjoyable time. I was now so depressed about Thailand that I was no fun to be with. Anne avoided me as best she could and spent more time with her sister.

One night I drank too much and nearly got into a fight with a bunch of locals. Anne had dragged me away in the end, preventing me from getting a beating. In the morning I felt even more depressed.

'You behaved like an arsehole last night Si,' Anne told me at breakfast.

'I'm fed up with this place,' I replied defensively. 'I don't like this country and I don't get on with the people.'

'Well I have been trying to tell you about that.'

Here it seemed one needed to be polite and follow a set of rituals in order to get things done. I had been barking blunt orders at people, with very limited success. I must have come across as very rude to everyone I met. Foolishly, I had stubbornly either refused or ignored Anne's advice.

Now I was really depressed. I whined out a list of further complaints, even though it was obvious that my negative thoughts were starting to get Anne down.

'I think it's best if I get out of here as quickly as possible,' I said finally.

'I think you're right,' Anne agreed.

It took some time, but I finally sorted out a return ticket to Perth. The flights were not as cheap as I had expected and I needed to borrow some money from Anne to complete my purchase.

In the end it was a huge relief to leave Anne and Helen in Thailand planning further travels together. Anne and I made vague plans to meet in Australia.

'I think it will do us good to have a break for a while,' she said before I went to catch a bus to the airport.

I could see that the life of a traveller was not for me. I had become bored. We had set ourselves a challenge while we were in Thailand which was not without difficulties, but I found an inevitability about the outcome. Perhaps for me the adventure was not complex enough, and for that reason did not have the uncertainty and excitement that I had come to associate with mountaineering expeditions. While there was obviously no shortage of risk and danger involved in what we were doing, there was something lacking. To me, what we were doing was not an adventure.

It was just getting light when I caught the airport bus into Perth. As the sun rose, high cloud streaked with pinks and reds formed a stunning backdrop to the skyscrapers of the city centre. The colours developed through a bewildering variety of shades. It was a remarkable dawn. Faced with such beauty, I felt the tensions of the previous months of climbing and travelling well up inside me. Suddenly, the stress released itself from my body and tears ran from my eyes and down my cheeks. It had taken me an event-filled nine months to reach Australia. I was looking forward to living normally for a while in a country with both taps and toilets, and where people spoke the same language as I did.

In the city centre I eagerly retrieved my rucksack from the trailer behind the bus and made my way to a telephone booth. With great excitement I picked up the receiver and dialled my brother's number. The telephone rang for a very long time before he answered.

'Fucking rude,' he stated bluntly.

It was six o'clock on a Saturday morning.

Chapter Six

Down Under

'Triple two, Simon.' The radio hanging from my belt crackled into life. 'Do you receive? Over.'

'Yeah,' I spluttered, trying to swallow a mouthful of sandwich and adding 'over' almost as an afterthought.

'Pick up at Anderson's Consulting, St Georges Terrace, going to West Perth. Call me once you've done it. Over and out.'

I hurriedly finished the sandwich and jumped on to my push-bike, before heading out of the quiet park and into the traffic of down-town Perth. My lunch break was over. I quickly reached the office block, dashed into the foyer and got into the lift. I stepped out on the tenth floor into the reception of Anderson's. A beautiful, immaculately dressed girl sat behind a sweeping wood and stainless steel desk at the far end of the spotless room. A few aboriginal paintings hung on the walls. As I walked towards her she picked up a phone.

'Your parcel is on its way,' she said, replacing the receiver.

A huge floor to ceiling window behind the desk gave stunning views across King's Park to the lake-like inlet of the Swan River around which the city of Perth is built. It was hard to know if I was supposed to stare at the girl or the view out of the window. I suddenly felt very conscious of my torn, faded Indian shorts and my sweat-soaked T-shirt.

I had been a cycle courier for two weeks. Having arrived in Australia with virtually no money I had to find a job quickly. To help me out my brother Matthew kindly lent me an old racing bike and laughed hysterically as I manically pedalled away from the house each morning to look for work. I followed several 'false leads and did a couple of days' labouring for a fencer before I found the cycling job. Having spent many of the previous months climbing and trekking, I was already fit and able to ride the bike quickly. It did not take long to learn the layout of the centre of Perth, as all the streets were in a simple grid-iron pattern, and the pick-ups and deliveries were usually between the same few companies. Each cyclist employed was paid a small retaining wage and then a fee for each delivery. The key to earning money was the number and speed of your deliveries. I soon got to learn the quickest ways between the different offices and the various short-cuts through walkways, shopping malls and parks. Further time could be saved by jumping red traffic lights, going the wrong way up one-way streets and cycling on the pavement. My brother caught a glimpse of me weaving through the city centre traffic one day and from then he referred to me as 'The Deadly Treadly.'

I had to suffer further ridicule from my work mates as the 'Triple Two' handle I was allotted had a chequered history. It seemed the last but one cyclist to hold the number had been knocked off his bike and spent a lengthy spell in hospital with a pair of broken legs. With even greater relish I was told that the previous incumbent had gone quite mad and was now being held in some sort of mental institution. I was not expected to last long.

While I adapted reasonably quickly to my work, I was still struggling to adjust to life back in the western world. The smart city offices of accountants, lawyers, advertising agencies and gold mining companies were in stark contrast to the squalor and deprivation that had been so evident in Asia. I was now mixing in a world where image was everything. The size, position, decoration, views and even the beauty of the receptionists at the offices I visited were meant to convey an image of wealth, power and status. I had spent the previous nine months moving among many people whose principal concern was finding the next meal, and to which image meant nothing. At times I found the visible opulence both shallow and sickening. It seemed so wasteful. One day I was hurrying along in the centre of Perth, when without thinking I paused, coughed up some phlegm and spat on to the pavement. Then almost instantaneously I squashed one nostril with my index finger and blew snot out of the other. I had not even considered the group of well-dressed secretaries walking towards me. The women stopped in their tracks, their faces filled with a mixture of horror and surprise.

'Charming!' one of the women eventually said.

I had completely forgotten that others found such behaviour offensive. My brother's girlfriend Stephanie prompted me to buy a new pair of shorts after I had been riding around for several days with a tear so large that it exposed most of my backside. I found beds too soft and so ended up sleeping under a sheet on the floor. Matthew found my whole lifestyle hilarious.

I felt like my life was in some sort of strange limbo. My adventures and travels had given me a different outlook and perspective from many other people. My moods swung violently. At first I felt depressed, but I became a little more positive once I managed to find work. However, I still did not feel like I belonged and as a result sometimes felt isolated and lonely. Occasionally I had tantalising flashes of perception which I considered profound, and at such moments I felt euphoric, as if I was on the verge of some major breakthrough in my own reasoning and development. Although that breakthrough never actually occurred.

Eventually my life settled into some sort of a rhythm. I went to work and cycled tirelessly around the city. With the help of a work mate's speedometer I calculated that I was averaging 100 kilometres each day. After the previous months of trekking and climbing the cycling toned my body, to a point where my physical fitness reached an unprecedented level. I made contact with the local climbing community and befriended a laid-back climber-cum-surfer called Peter Cox. We got on well, were of similar rock-climbing ability and made occasional outings to the small outcrops in the hills outside Perth, as well as some weekends away further down the coast to the granite sea cliffs of Willyabrup and West Cape Howe. On Thursday nights I joined my work mates for happy hour in a pub near the company offices, and on Fridays I hit the town with Matthew and Stephanie, or their Irish lodger Brenda.

'Compared with other people we've had staying, you've settled in the easiest,' Matthew complimented me one day.

It seemed my ability to adapt, which had deserted me in Thailand and marred my time there, had returned.

My sister Sarah arrived from Britain, and for the first time since we were children we were all reunited under a single roof. It was nice to be a group of siblings again with our own particular blend of friendly rivalry, ridicule, humour and love.

Yet however comforting my surroundings were, I was still far from settled. As soon as my life fell into any sort of routine I became bored. Life without the prospect of an adventure in the not too distant future was now impossible. I replied to a letter Sean had sent me and accepted an invitation to join him and Mike Searle on an expedition to Pakistan later in the summer. The chance to visit another region of the Karakoram was too big to turn down. When I spoke to Anne and told her of my plans over the telephone, once she had arrived in Sydney, there was a frosty silence. With the decision taken, my immediate future again had some direction. I had dreams to think about and plan for, while I went about my day-to-day routine. All I had to do was find the money. The fact that I managed to save precious little of my meagre wage each week seemed of little consequence. Something would turn up. It always had in the past.

'Quick, Simon,' Matthew burst into the kitchen, where I was helping cook the dinner. He looked unusually excited. 'Mum's on the phone.'

I wondered what all the fuss was about. My parents occasionally telephoned at weekends, and then they usually spoke to my brother. Why were they ringing up on a weekday to speak to me?

'Everybody's been trying to get hold of you,' she explained.

'Who, Mum?'

'Newspapers, radio, television, the lot. You could have had a field day if you'd been here.'

'What do they want to talk about?'

'Joe's book.'

'Oh, you mean *Touching the Void*?'

'Yes. That's it.'

It seemed that the book, which had been published the previous summer in Britain, had been received very well. I had read a manuscript just before leaving and thought little more about it. So far I had been grateful for a few small cheques that had come my way for the inclusion of some of my photographs in the book, which had helped prolong my travels to Australia. Other than that it had had little effect on me. The book had recently been published in the States, and now it seemed that some Hollywood film company were interested in making a piece about our adventures in Peru.

To me the whole thing seemed like fantasy, but I spoke to Joe in Britain who seemed to be taking it all very seriously. Then a production assistant made a series of calls to me from California. They wanted me to go to Canada to reconstruct our epic and to be interviewed on camera. They were prepared to pay very well for this. Matthew drove me to the office of the mining company he worked for to send several fax messages. Finally, a deal was struck and I sent off the signed contract and release forms. A few days later an air ticket arrived from a rather up-market travel agent in the centre of Perth. I was going to be flown first class across Australia and the Pacific to Los Angeles, and then up to Calgary in Canada for three days of filming in the nearby Bugaboo Mountains, before being flown all the way back again. I could hardly believe my luck.

In a remarkable eight-day round trip I left the end of the southern summer for the early northern spring. In Los Angeles, I missed a flight connection and so spent a night with the production assistant in the centre of Hollywood, after an afternoon on Venice Beach. Then in Calgary I met Joe, along with his friend John Stevenson. It seemed strange to be meeting them in such circumstances – me with my deep tan and bleached hair alongside their pallid skin. Our skin colour was not the only difference. Since I had left Britain Joe's life had changed. He had been catapulted from unemployed climber to successful author virtually overnight. I could sense he was enjoying the money and power his new position in life brought, but at the same time he did not want to become alienated from the community of climbers he had lived among for so many years. Many wonderful things were happening in his life that were not happening to those around him and people were envious.

The three days of filming from helicopters in the beautiful unspoilt mountains were a mixture of laughter and tears. We laughed at the excesses of the Hollywood film production company, who at one point actually flew ham and tomato sandwiches from one location to another because the producer preferred them to the sandwiches at that site. Then we laughed at each other as I reenacted the rope cutting incident and Joe his dramatic fall, and we laughed at the assistants shovelling snow into huge fans to create a blizzard. The drunken evenings in local bars always started jovially enough, but eventually wound their way back tearfully to the guilt and bewilderment Joe felt from all of his instant success. With my own mind lodged on another continent far away, and having little idea of what had happened at home, I found it impossible to offer much in the way of advice or support. To me, what had occurred in Peru four years previously already seemed very distant, but I wondered if Joe, through writing his book, and the media attention it had created, was reliving those very traumatic experiences.

Our time together passed in a blur and all too soon we were saying our goodbyes. Flying back, I crossed the date line for the second time in less than a week, and stayed a night in Sydney before continuing on to Perth. The following day I was back on the streets with my cycle.

Anne had arrived in Australia a few weeks earlier, but had gone to the eastern side of the country to rock-climb before the onset of winter. We had not parted on the best of terms and my decision to return to Pakistan had done little to heal the rift. Yet despite our problems I dearly wanted to see her again. The fact that she was climbing at Mount Arapiles – a place I had dreamt of visiting for many years – only increased that desire.

With $3000 on its way as payment for the filming in Canada, I had little need to continue working, so I handed in my notice and began to plan how to get across Australia. As I had plenty of time it seemed unnecessary to buy an expensive air ticket to Adelaide or Melbourne. For a few days I seriously considered cycling, but abandoned the idea because I did not want to take panniers full of weighty climbing equipment. However, I wanted to see something of the country and the people in it, so in the end I settled for my usual form of transport when I was at home – hitch-hiking.

'Here, step in this, kid,' Doug Scott said, linking his hands together and putting them down by his waist. We were about a hundred metres up an unclimbed crack-line on the granite sea cliffs of West Cape Howe. It was my lead and I had been trying to get off the ledge unsuccessfully for about five minutes. Doug had taken pity on me. I gratefully put a foot into his waiting hands and he hoisted me upwards to a point where the crack I had been attempting to climb widened enough to accept my hands. I shoved them deep inside the fissure and pulled my thumbs down across my palms to wedge them in place. Then I pulled myself up and placed my feet lower down the same crack.

It was nice to see Doug again, visiting Perth to give a lecture, and to spend a weekend climbing with him in such a dramatic setting. The trip would also act as a spring-board for my journey east, as once the climbing was over I planned to start hitching in the nearby town of Albany.

The crack gently overhung and I moved quickly, knowing my strength would not last long on such ground. It was hot and humid and I instantly felt overdressed in my fleece clothing. Sweat poured from my skin and I felt crystals tearing into the flesh on the back of my hands. Somehow I hung on, placed a metal wedge in the crack, clipped the rope to it and moved up to reach some large, incut holds. I monkeyed out rightwards, deeply aware of the huge swell crashing into the base of the cliffs far below, and with the last of my strength, pulled myself on to a small rounded ledge. It accommodated only one foot at a time, but at least I was in balance. By carefully moving my hands and feet around I managed to rest my arms.

'Well done kid,' floated up from below.

After a few minutes of shuffling on the ledge I was ready to go again. Somehow I powered my way up an overhanging corner and turned a small roof, before wedging myself into a narrow chimney. The difficult climbing was over. Thrutching up the chimney to the top was awkward and strenuous, but I never felt that I was going to fall. With a final heave I pulled myself on to level ground and lay panting on the rocky shelf. I removed my jacket and instantly felt sweat wicking away from my T-shirt in the light breeze that was blowing over the top of the cliffs. I soon began to cool down.

I moved back from the edge and belayed in some bushes. Then I heaved up the spare rope and yelled down to Doug to start climbing, before reclining and enjoying the evening's watery sunshine. There were cliffs in both directions for many kilometres, forming small bays separated by impressive headlands. Lines of perfect rollers stretched out into the ocean and crashed into the base of the cliffs with metronomic regularity. The power of the waves was truly frightening. Although it was a calm day, we had been forced to start our climb twenty metres above the waterline as the waves often rode that far up the cliffs. Peter Cox had told me that on one occasion he had watched waves ride the entire height of the crags and blow over the top.

To me the cliffs seemed like a huge adventure playground, and yet they had hardly been climbed on. The possibilities for new climbs were almost infinite. At home a cliff of such size and potential would have been spotted many years before and worked out. Only the most difficult of lines would remain. Here the tiny population of climbers were spoilt for choice and preferred to climb nearer to Perth, where most of them lived. As a modest rock climber, the opportunities for exploratory climbing made me excited and giddy.

Doug's bearded face soon appeared over the top of the cliff.

'What a place,' he said through a beaming smile. Then he walked towards me, generously holding out his hand. I stood up and shook it. As we walked along the cliff tops back to where the jeep was parked the sun burst out from beneath a bank of cloud, bathing us in beautiful golden light. Later, as the sun began to set, both the sea and the clouds turned the same outrageous shades of pink, orange and mauve that it seemed as if one was a reflection of the other. It was a fitting end to a perfect day.

'Take it easy mate,' said Peter Cox, as I climbed out of

his jeep the following morning. I had enjoyed his company over the previous months and our weekend climbing trips away. Now, as often was the case I had befriended someone only to say goodbye to them a short time later.

I dragged out my rucksack, shook hands with him and waved goodbye as I crossed the road to the junction of the Esperance road. As I watched Pete drive off into the distance towards Perth, a little doubt crept into my mind. For a few moments I wondered if I was making a mistake, but quickly banished such negative thoughts.

An hour later I was still at the junction. Only two vehicles had passed me and one of the drivers had indicated he was only going a short way. Doubts began to creep back. It was not too late to give up, catch a bus back to Perth and arrange some transport from there. I was seriously considering the prospect, when a car turned on to the Esperance road and stopped as I put my thumb out. I was off.

The day passed pleasantly in the end. With two lifts I reached the town of Esperance, where after a fish-and-chip supper, I bedded down in a ditch for the night. In the morning a rep picked me up almost immediately and said he could take me through to Norseman – the last settlement in Western Australia. He insisted on stopping at regular intervals to show me elaborate water-collection systems that had been built by convicts to supply the steam trains from Esperance to Norseman. Even with the detours we made Norseman by lunchtime.

The next lift was crucial. Between Norseman and Port Augusta to the west of Adelaide lay the Nullabor Plain – a vast expanse of virtually uninhabited scrubland. I needed to get a lift with someone going right across. I did not want to get stranded at a junction to a cattle station out in the middle of it all.

I positioned myself by a filling station where everyone was topping up and stuck my thumb out. It began to rain, a little at first, then torrentially. I retreated under the canopy of the petrol station and started simply asking people for a lift across. Nobody was interested, and when I went inside to buy some food and drink, the attendant told me how dry the town usually was. At dusk I gave up and walked off through the trees towards a derelict-looking property, hoping for a roof over my head for the night. Then suddenly I hit something. Lying on the ground, I shook my head feeling dazed. There was a bleeding gash on my nose. I pulled my head torch from my rucksack and turned it on. I had walked into a head-high strand of barbed wire. Giving up on the derelict house I walked back to the filling station and found a Portacabin to crawl under for the night. It rained into the early hours.

A visit to the toilet in the morning confirmed my fears. During the night a congealed lump of blood had formed on my nose and my eyes had blackened. I looked like I had been in a fight. It was not going to help me get a lift.

The first few people I asked that morning looked worried as I approached them and brushed aside my requests dismissively. I resigned myself to a long day. Then I noticed a truck driver round the side of the station cleaning the windows of his wagon. I walked towards him.

'Are you going across?' I asked.

'Yeah,' he nodded.

'Any chance of a lift?'

'No worries mate,' he said with a nasal twang. 'Name's Kevin.'

'Simon,' I replied, barely able contain my delight.

I climbed up the set of steps and made myself comfortable inside the huge cab. We set off. The truck was ponderous, taking minutes and numerous gear changes to reach a cruising speed. Once it did, I felt like nothing would stop it.

'Where you going?' Kevin asked once we got up to speed.

I thought about the question momentarily and settled for a town on the nearest main road to Arapiles.

'Horsham.'

'I'll drop you there.'

This was perfect. My lift was going to take me 2,500 kilometres and drop me thirty kilometres from where I wanted to be. I could hardly believe my luck. The eighteen-hour wait had been worth it after all.

Kevin explained that he had driven from Brisbane to Perth and was now on his way to Melbourne. There was nothing puzzling in this, except that his schedule seemed to include almost no sleep.

The road was slightly undulating but monotonously straight, and passed through sparsely wooded bush that never seemed to vary from one hour to the next. Occasionally wedge-tailed eagles took to the air from dead kangaroos lying at the side of the road.

'For the roos,' Kevin remarked pointing at the windscreen, as we passed the first carcass. The window itself was covered in wire mesh and the lower part of the truck's front protected by substantial iron bars. The message was clear. Kevin did not even attempt to avoid kangaroos. To keep himself entertained he chatted on a CB radio and pulled a string attached to an air horn as trucks passed in the opposite direction.

'D'ya fancy a carrot?' he asked at lunchtime.

'Why not,' I replied hesitantly, somewhat baffled by his question.

Moments later Kevin stopped the truck, jumped out and after opening up the trailer returned carrying an armful of the biggest carrots I have ever seen. For a while, we sat eating the ridiculously sized vegetables and waving them out of the window at oncoming vehicles.

When we dropped down on to the ancient seabed that forms the Nullabor Plain, nearly all the trees disappeared. I had never seen anywhere quite so flat, empty and barren. All that interrupted the view were service stations roughly every 300 kilometres.

Kevin drove without a break all day, before pulling in at a service station just before nightfall. Then, after just a two-hour break we left. Later, Kevin began to get tired. I became seriously worried when he started falling asleep at the wheel.

'Wake up!' I shouted, as the truck drifted to the other side of the road.

With a startled look Kevin opened his eyes and steered the wagon back to the correct side of the road. This seemed to be a turning point. Kevin asked me to pass him a particular cassette box and opened it up. There were pills inside. He swallowed some. Half an hour later his eyes were wide open and his pupils massively dilated. He was rambling manically, driving with his head almost on the windscreen. I stayed awake for as long as I could and then drifted off into a nervous sleep.

When I woke Kevin was on the CB. Later, we stopped in a layby and after a short break another truck pulled up. Kevin returned clutching more pills, and after swallowing another handful he started driving again. It began to get light. This was madness. Kevin had been driving for nearly twenty-four hours while I had been with him, with only a two-hour break. He had not slept.

As we drove along, Kevin explained the rules under which the truckers operated. Each state had different laws. In some you were required to fill in a log book of hours worked, in others not, and once you passed from one state to another, you could begin again. The whole system encouraged abuse and allowed the truck drivers to work insane hours. To me it seemed that the states and government were turning a blind eye, so that goods could be transported around such a vast country cheaply.

Kevin loved his life on the open road – a life filled with excitement, risk and adventure. In some ways it was similar to my own. What was different was that his lifestyle was an acceptable occupation, whereas many consider mountaineering at best unjustified and at worst quite mad. People regularly call for climbing to be tightly controlled or even banned. If I had an accident in the mountains I might hurt myself and possibly my partner, but I would not hurt members of the wider public. Yet Kevin was allowed and even encouraged to operate in a manner that was both dangerous to himself and others. In the night we had passed a jack-knifed truck on the longest section of straight road in the world. I suspected why it had happened.

The second helping of pills made Kevin a little incoherent. The third made him psychotic. During the morning we stopped for drinks and he explained that in South Australia bottles and cans all carried a deposit to encourage recycling. He thought this was a good idea. Shortly afterwards we entered the State of Victoria and Kevin insisted on hurling all the bottles and cans out of the window as the deposit was no longer valid.

'How long are you going to keep driving for?' I asked him as we neared Horsham.

'Till the doctor tells me to stop,' came the blunt reply.

We shook hands when Kevin finally reached Horsham and I stood dazed as the truck pulled away and drove off into the distance. We had covered the 2,500 kilometres in thirty-three hours. Kevin had only stopped on three occasions and his breaks had amounted to no more than three hours. As lifts go, it had been a very good one.

By the time I reached the campsite at Arapiles I was in a state of excitement. I dumped my kit and made my way up through the trees to a place where I had been told Anne was climbing. Greg Cunningham's voice led me to the spot. When I reached him, Anne was just completing the pitch above. We both knew Greg from home. He insisted that I second the pitch and I hurriedly put on his harness and boots. Then, climbing as fast as possible I dashed up the route, lunging the last few moves to where Anne was sitting. I knew immediately something was wrong. She would not look me in the eye and turned away as I went to kiss her.

We shared a tent that night, but the atmosphere was edgy.

'I'm not intense about anything at the moment, Si,' Anne said, when I tried to engage her in conversation.

We avoided each other for much of the following day.

'As far as I'm concerned, our relationship is over,' Anne told me that night, before moving to another tent.

We had not been getting on well before I left Thailand, but I had thought our time apart would help. In a sense it had. It had helped Anne to decide to finish our relationship. Despite the few frosty conversations we had exchanged by telephone since Anne's arrival in Australia, I had blindly held the belief that all would be well. The reality hit me hard. I was heartbroken as the dreams I had built up in my mind about a life together were shattered.

I tried to stay busy, and threw myself into climbing and the colourful campsite life, but it was difficult. Arapiles was a place I had visited in my mind for many years. I had read numerous articles about climbing on its perfect orange quartzite cliffs. The place had acquired a mythical status in my mind. It was somewhere I associated with pleasure and joy. Now that myth had been destroyed. It did not help that the summer was coming to an end and the campsite's long-time residents were gradually drifting away. As people left, they discarded food, tents and furniture accumulated during their lengthy stays. However, the collection of armchairs, settees and plastic shelters that remained seemed soulless without their rightful occupants. It reminded me of Snell's Field in Chamonix at the end of an Alpine season. The days were getting shorter and the nights colder. The place began to take on an air of decay, which only exaggerated my own feelings.

When the rains came I escaped to the nearby Grampian Mountains, but there was no let-up and after a few days spent around a fire in a cave at the bottom of some cliffs I drifted into Melbourne and then on to Canberra.

There I stayed with Craig Kentwell, whom I had not seen since my first visit to Pakistan three years earlier. He was the perfect host.

'Here's the washing machine and here's my car and bike keys,' Craig said, pointing each out as I entered his house.

Craig took the car to work, and for many of the following ten days I went out on his motorbike. The 550cc machine was big and heavy compared to the tiny bike that Anne and I had used in Thailand, but it did have one great advantage – speed. At first I drove the bike very cautiously, but it did not take long to get used to it. By the time Craig's holidays came round I was driving the bike flat-out, and it was perhaps fortuitous that we left to tour some climbing areas in northern New South Wales and Queensland before I had an accident.

Over two weeks, we wound our way gently northwards in Craig's car and climbed in some wonderful, isolated places. In the wooded campsites kookaburras darted down from tree branches and removed the fillings from half-finished sandwiches, and at night the glow of the camp fire illuminated the huge eyes of the possums. Flocks of startlingly bright birds flew across the fields and each succeeding evening the sunset seemed to be more outrageously colourful than the last. Outside the small towns that we visited to collect supplies, we rarely saw other people. And yet the empty beauty of the places we visited only seemed to exaggerate my feeling of loneliness. By the time we returned to Canberra, I was happy to start making my way back to Western Australia to catch my flight back to Bangkok.

I had gone to Australia thinking that I might stay and make it my home. There had seemed precious little to keep me in Britain, where I had no house and little in the way of work. Now I was not so sure. For an outdoor person like myself Australia possessed wilderness in abundance. Many of the wildest and most beautiful parts of the country were owned by the state and access to them was guaranteed. There was no danger of some angry landowner turning up and throwing you off the land. And, unlike in Britain, there was little you could possibly break or damage. Therefore, you seemed to be able to enjoy the wilderness without too many annoying restrictions. The downside was that many places were so remote, dry or inaccessible that you would never even consider a visit.

Yet despite liking many of the places I had visited, there was something about Australia that I was not comfortable with, and it was not until I started my journey back to Perth that I realised what it was. In Britain we are surrounded by old buildings, roads and monuments and when you look at the land you can see that people have been cultivating and managing it for thousands of years. This gave an undefinable feeling, like a soul, to the land at home. I knew that there was a long-established aboriginal culture in Australia, but it was a very different culture to my own and it had not made the marked impact on the landscape that I was familiar with. As a result, in Australia I felt no connection with the past and as such could not bond with the land. I was surprised to discover how strong this feeling was, and wondered if it was the same for others. Many of the people I met in Australia who had emigrated there were full of praise for the place, but to me it all felt rather soulless.

It was good to spend a few more days with my brother and sister, and to see my parents, who were also visiting for the first time in over a year. I had been in Australia for more than four eventful months and I had been fortunate to visit so many places in such a vast country, but I knew my heart lay elsewhere. I left happy to be returning to the mountains in Pakistan, but felt sad about saying goodbye to my family and wondered when I would see my brother again.

I was only in Bangkok for two nights and one full day.

'You seem much more relaxed than before,' the girl in the travel agents' who had sold me the ticket to Australia told me. I felt even more relaxed after I had bought a ticket to Karachi.

I got off the plane in Pakistan smiling. The heat, filth and smells felt like a home-coming. I dealt with the intimidating rush of taxi drivers outside the airport as if they were an everyday occurrence.

I caught up with Sean in Gilgit. He had been travelling and taking photographs in China. Two days later Mike

Searle rolled into town in the Leicester University jeep, still listing badly to one side. I felt flattered that they had asked me to join them, and our faith in each other had been such that only a couple of letters had been exchanged to arrange the whole expedition. But it was perhaps inevitable that something would go seriously wrong. The road to Skardu was broken by a massive landslide, and although we did not have to pass through Skardu to get into the mountains, our supply of high-altitude cooking gas had been transported to the town. It took ten days to reopen the road.

Eventually we retrieved the gas, drove to a roadhead, walked in and set up a base camp. Bitanmal, on the side of the Hispar Glacier, was a special place, with amazing panoramas of the surrounding mountains, but our trip was not blessed with good luck.

Initially the weather was bad, although we did manage to struggle to the top of an unnamed mountain we could hardly see in the almost white-out conditions. Then Sean and I attempted a stunning unclimbed peak further up the valley, but were forced to retreat after two nights spent hanging in our sleeping bags in an avalanche-filled couloir that had drenched us to the skin. On the walk back to camp Sean wrecked the ligaments in his right knee. He could do no more climbing.

The twelve days of uninterrupted perfect weather were very frustrating for me. I made a very nice outing with Mike to climb a further small peak, but he did not possess the technical skills to accompany me on a more challenging objective.

We passed the remainder of our time by visiting the Rupal Face of Nanga Parbat on our way out of the mountains, hoping to get a glimpse of the world's largest mountain face. Somehow it seemed a fitting end to my time away. I stood in silence gazing with awe at the 5,000 metres of mountain that soared above me, knowing that several parties of mountaineers had climbed to the top. Although I struggled to imagine a climb of such magnitude, it inspired me.

We made our way back down the now familiar mountain roads to the plains of the Punjab. I bought a further ticket home and set off on the train.

By the time I reached the airport in Karachi I had run out of money. I did not even have enough to pay the departure tax. Luckily, a customs officer took pity on me and paid. The airline were less sympathetic.

'That is sixty-six pounds in excess baggage sir,' the airline representative said at the check-in. 'How would you like to pay?'

'I can't.'

'In that case you must leave some of your baggage, or miss the flight.'

I waited until everyone had checked in and then tried again. The Pakistani staff were sympathetic and I think that if it had been left up to them they would have let me on the plane. The problem was a Kuwait Airlines official who was playing by the rules. He was completely unmoved by my increasingly desperate pleas. As the staff started to close the check-in I began to consider what to leave behind. Then I had a brainwave.

'Can I pay with a cheque?'

The official agreed to let me pay this way once we reached London. I had to hand my passport to the cabin crew as security when I entered the plane. When we arrived at Heathrow a message came over the tannoy telling me to contact the ground staff as I left the plane.

An official was waiting for me with my passport and a fax from Karachi. He took me into a small room.

'I would like a cheque for sixty-six pounds, Mr Yates.'

'Well, you can't have one.'

'In Karachi you told us you would pay here,' he said, waving the fax, his face filling with blood.

'I lied.'

The official screamed at me, but in the end they had to return my passport. Then he said he would keep my bags, but it was a hollow threat. The bags appeared on the carousel and I loaded them on to a trolley and wheeled them away, waving a defiant finger at the official.

'Welcome home, Simon,' I thought, when I eventually made it into the arrivals hall.

Chapter Seven

On the Ropes

I returned to Sheffield and after a few days of shuffling around friends' houses and sleeping on floors, I found some more permanent accommodation. John and Alison Corbett were a nice couple, whose first baby was just a few weeks old. Alison worked as a physiotherapist, but they needed a lodger to bring in some extra money while John was studying to become a teacher.

Compared to some of the squalid all-male houses I had shared in the past, the place seemed like a palace. Having spent so much time in Asia and now being a little older, I found my perspectives had changed. I knew now just how lucky I had been to be born in Britain and the advantages I enjoyed as a result of that. Regardless of how much money I earned, I had access to clean water and sanitation, health care and an array of other public services. In addition, I was able to use a vast transport and telecommunications infrastructure to do things more easily. Now I knew all too well how difficult life was for people in other parts of the world who did not have access to all these things. However, it was the spirit I had seen in people while I was away, their will to try to provide for themselves and their families, that inspired me the most to make changes in my life. As I came from a privileged background in a rich country, I now felt the least I could do was to try and adopt that spirit. After years of living on benefits and some brief odd-jobs, I had become determined to support myself.

I always found it awkward to adjust to life at home after I had been away, but this time was much more difficult. Previously, my longest trips had only involved a matter of two or three months. Then I usually found that my own thinking had altered more than people's at home, and that the place I had left had not changed physically.

But in the year and a half I had been away, roads had been built, huge buildings erected, businesses opened and closed. Friends had moved, got jobs and changed them, bought houses and had children. The scale of the changes took some time to sink in. I often found myself having feelings of déjà vu, as if I had visited a place, or had been involved in a situation before. Things felt familiar, but not quite right, like when you suddenly remember you dreamed of a similar thing just the night before.

In many ways catching up with individual people was the simplest. If I spent time with them, looked at their new circumstances and asked questions, I could become a part of their lives again. What was more difficult to deal with were the changes in society as a whole. At times I felt like a stranger in my own land.

What was immediately noticeable was how much more expensive everything was. The money that I had sent back from the filming in Canada was not going to last long. However, there seemed to be a lot more money about and the gloom, decay and recession that had hung over Sheffield since I first moved there in the early 1980s finally seemed to have lifted. Everything suddenly seemed bright and new. Even some of the vast areas of derelict steel works on the east side of the city, that had stood with 'to let' or 'for sale' signs above them for as long as I could remember, were being redeveloped. But I sensed that along with all the commercial activity people's attitudes had changed – their lives appeared to be much more focused on money. The shift from heavy industry and manufacturing into service industries had continued unabated. Now, it appeared, we all sold each other pensions, holidays, insurance and cream teas to have while we were on holiday. It seemed that Britain no longer made anything.

I soon realised, however, that climbers as a group had benefited from some of the changes that had been taking place. For many years rock climbing and mountaineering had been a minority sport practised by a small group of devoted enthusiasts, supplied with equipment by a tiny group of outdoor retailers and manufacturers. The sport supported just a few people working for these businesses and as outdoor instructors and guides. Their numbers had been rising steadily, but were still small. Now suddenly all that had changed.

Perhaps climbing simply fitted into the thinking of the time, with its emphasis on the individual and risk-taking in business. Under such circumstances I could see how climbing worked as a powerful cultural metaphor, where people took personal risks to reach the top. If just a few years earlier the public perceived climbing as an odd activity practised by a strange group of drably dressed bearded men, now it seemed they saw it as dynamic, athletic and glamorous. Climbing had become sexy.

The numbers of people going out to the crags, and visiting the indoor climbing walls being built all over the country, had rocketed. Even the numbers involved in more specialist branches of the sport, such as winter climbing and alpinism, were increasing. Sales of equipment and clothing soared with the numbers of those participating, as did opportunities for working in the new and expanding businesses.

Now, looking back, I could see the roots of all this popularity. In the early 1980s there had been literally thousands of unemployed climbers living in communities from Bristol to Fort William, their only limiting factor being the proximity of good climbing. It had been this group of enthusiasts that had created the publicity and interest that had led to wider public awareness and participation. Yet these people took part simply because of their passion for the sport, fuelled by the lack of employment opportunities at that time. Now with a twist of wonderful irony, many of those enthusiasts had been absorbed into the businesses that their actions had helped to create. A whole generation of people, acting out their dreams and following a passion, had in effect created their own jobs. It made me realise that if enough people did something, with enough conviction, for a long enough period of time, then others would follow and ultimately businesses would grow up around that activity.

Friends and associates, who for years had lived in squalor and poverty, were now driving around in fast new cars, paid for by sponsorship deals with companies or winnings from climbing-wall competitions that were now taking place. Even more were working for clothing and equipment companies, and there were others building climbing walls.

Climbing was now so popular that it was regularly covered by articles in the mainstream press and climbers even featured in lifestyle magazines. Climbers, who for years had struggled to find a girlfriend because of their scruffiness, poverty and lack of social skills, were now appearing on lists of Britain's most eligible bachelors. I vowed to get my hands on a modest amount of some of the money that seemed to be flowing around.

'Right, can I have your attention?'

Mike Woolridge sat at the head of the large table and as head guide was about to begin his nightly briefing. It was the start of the second week of winter skills courses organised by Mal Duff, based at a large house outside Spean Bridge in the heart of the Scottish Highlands.

I had enjoyed working for Mal in the past. He had a fairly relaxed approach to guiding, and tended to employ people on the grounds of experience and ability rather than paper qualifications. For this reason he always seemed to get reasonable clients, who basically wanted to get as much climbing done as possible. Most of the other guides were friends and generally we were left to make our own decisions about where we went and what we did. Sometimes by the end of each week it was more like going climbing with a couple of friends than working. This year, however, it was different. The weather was being particularly unkind. It had been warm and wet for weeks and higher up huge quantities of wet snow had accumulated, which was now avalanching off the wet grass beneath.

I listened to the briefing without much interest. We would all go together to somewhere near Bauchaille Etive Mor – a beautiful mountain at the head of Glencoe – and do some winter skills practice low down on a gently angled hillside that was deemed safe from avalanches. It would involve more wallowing in thigh-deep snow, followed by some lessons on technique. We would be back for lunchtime and spend the afternoon drinking coffee in the Nevisport Cafe in Fort William.

When the briefing ended one of the clients took me to one side.

'Look,' he said. 'It was really cramped in that minibus today. I'm going to take my car tomorrow. Do you want to come along? We'll be able to smoke without bothering the others.'

'Count me in,' I replied, before heading off to my room.

In the morning I strolled into the kitchen silently, just as most of the others were finishing their breakfasts. It was 5.30 and as usual I was not enjoying the early start. I shoved a piece of toast into my mouth and made a coffee, which I struggled to drink. It was time to leave. I put on my plastic boots and reluctantly walked to the car.

'Do you mind if I come along as well?' Henry Todd asked, looking towards the crowded minibus.

'I don't see why not,' I replied. 'So long as you can put up with the smoke.'

'I'm sure it will be more comfortable than in that bus.'

I nodded my agreement. Henry, a fellow guide working for Mal, was a huge man and I remembered him squashing into the front seat of the bus the previous day.

'Looks like a better day,' I said as we drove towards Fort William. 'You can actually see the Ben.' For the first time in days Ben Nevis's huge North Face was virtually free of cloud. Only the very top was covered.

'Good,' Henry sighed. 'I'm getting fed up with this crap weather.'

'Yes we could do with some frosts. The only ice I've seen in Scotland this winter has been in gin and tonics.'

We drove on through the almost deserted streets of Fort William, following the minibus in front and then wound along the shores of Loch Linnhe. It was a stunning morning. Weak, watery sunshine flickered through the trees and bathed the mountains in light, the reflections of which rippled in the loch below. Occasionally, we passed through small pockets of mist that swirled around like smoke. On such rare mornings in Scotland in the winter, it was easy to forget the usual wind and the driving rain. This beauty was my reason for coming back.

We all sat in silence admiring the views as we crossed the Ballachulish Bridge and began to anticipate the drive up Glencoe. Then, as we left Glencoe village, disaster struck.

'Oh God,' I heard Henry scream, as we watched the minibus in front spin 180 degrees, mount the nearside verge and nose-dive into an enormous ditch. The bus then bounced off the far wall of the ditch and spun round further so its front was now facing us. As it did so, Jon Tinker's head came crashing through the windscreen.

Moments later we hit the ice. The back of the car spun one way then the other, but we kept going forward and the vehicle quickly regained traction. As soon as we came to a halt Henry was out of the door. I followed him up the road, surprised that we were both skating on the glassy surface. By the time I had caught up with him, he had wrestled open the back doors of the minibus. I had not really thought what would be inside, but the sight was shocking. Most of the seats had sheared off their mountings and were lying along with their occupants in a pile behind the front seats. One client climbed out immediately, but the rest lay groaning. Mike Woolridge, who had been driving, seemed very distressed. Henry jumped in and started trying to push his way to the front.

'I'm coming Mike,' he shouted, trying to tear the front seat out.

'Just calm down,' I screamed, now suddenly aware that unless we removed the debris and everyone inside in a careful, systematic manner we would end up hurting people more. 'Let's do this slowly.'

Gradually we worked our way forwards, taking out rucksacks, plastic boots, ice-axes and seats as we needed and then helping people outside. Someone went for an ambulance and others stopped to help. We cleared the back of the minibus and then managed to get the driver's door open and extract Mike Woolridge, who was trapped behind the steering wheel. Fortunately, there were lots of spare warm clothes, space-blankets and sleeping bags in the rucksacks to cover the people now laid out on the verge. It was going to be more difficult to remove Jon Tinker, who was still trapped, semi-conscious, in the passenger seat. He sat slumped, gently moaning, with his face swelling grotesquely. We put a jacket over him and left him where he was. Of the nine inside, only one had escaped injury. There were a lot of broken bones, along with gashed and bruised faces.

It was hard to know how long everything took, but a policeman arrived first and took one look at the carnage, before marching away to tend to the traffic. Then the ambulances came — four in total. More police turned up and finally a helicopter ambulance from Inverness landed in the field next to the minibus. We were later told that a fire tender had also been sent, but had spun off the road on some black ice before it reached us. The whole convoy was slowly loaded up and then headed back for Fort William. Suddenly everyone had gone and Henry and I were left, standing dazed at the side of the road. The ice had now gone.

It was easy to figure out what had happened. After raining nearly all night the skies had cleared a little before dawn and there had been a couple of hours of frost. The water lying on the untreated roads had frozen and the minibus had hit a patch of it. We packed all the remaining gear and drove to Fort William.

We relaxed a little on the journey into town, safe in the knowledge that all would receive the medical care they needed. However, we received a shock when we entered the hospital. The small numbers of staff in the casualty department were struggling to deal with the influx. Henry and I spent the morning being porters, pushing people in beds and wheelchairs in and out of the X-ray department and around different wards.

That evening, back at the house, I sat with Henry sharing a bottle of wine.

'What made you come with us this morning?' I asked.

'I don't really know. I was walking towards the minibus and just didn't like the look of it.'

'Well it was a lucky call.'

Henry laughed, well aware of how close he had been to climbing into the seat that Jon had taken. I had always known that climbing was dangerous. However, the accident made me realise that driving on icy roads, along Asian jeep tracks, in third-world buses and taking mountain flights were all hazardous in their own right. The risks associated with the travel that I undertook to go climbing had seemed so small that I had not even considered them. The minibus accident had changed all that.

'It's ironic why I wasn't in the bus,' I said smiling.

'Because you smoke,' Henry sniggered.

'Yes. They don't put that on the side of cigarette packets do they?'

Many drivers and smokers consider climbing an unjustifiable risk. But on this occasion one proven high-risk pastime had saved me from injury caused by something recognised as less risky.

Winter passed into spring and once again my money began to run low. Doug Scott had invited me to Pakistan in the summer and I had already arranged to go to Shivling in India for the autumn. If I was to have any chance of going away, I needed to find work. Word was spreading that climbers and cavers were being snapped up by newly-formed access companies. It seemed that our skills on ropes were being put to use in the construction of office blocks, which were sprouting up across central London as fast as developers could build them. To unemployed climbers the sums of money involved seemed like fortunes, and there were stories of people financing year-long trips from just a couple of months' work on the right job.

'You need to go and see Pete Robinson,' someone told me.

I made my way down the Abbeydale Road in Sheffield and eventually located his offices above an Indian restaurant. The smartness inside seemed strangely at odds with the humble exterior. Compared with the offices I had seen in Perth this was modest, but the people inside carried the same air of purpose and I could sense that they were working in a busy, successful business.

The offices were open-plan and I quickly guessed from the amount of attention he was receiving that it was Pete at a desk in the corner. Eventually he waved me over. I waited some time while he finished a telephone call. Then he looked at me while rolling a cigarette.

'So, you'll be another one of those climbers who's never done a day's work in their lives?' he said, lighting the cigarette.

'Yeah, I suppose I am.' There seemed little point in arguing with him.

'Well you've just got lucky.'

'In what way?'

'The lads say you're okay. So I'll see you right.'

'Pardon?'

'I'll put some money in your back pocket.'

As I began to understand Pete's sound-bite form of speaking I found it increasingly difficult to keep a straight face. I could not quite tell if he was being serious, ironic or sarcastic, whether he was ridiculing me or himself. By now, other people in the office had gathered round and solemnly nodded in agreement at the end of each statement.

'Scaffolder me,' he continued, 'since I left school. Now look at me,' he waved his arms expansively.

I nodded and tried to look impressed. His big hooked nose, short trimmed beard, permanent grin and way of talking combined to make him seem comical.

'This is a new business this,' Pete announced thoughtfully. 'It's got a big future. Get yourself one of these and keep all your receipts for the tax man,' he pointed to a stack of papers speared on a wire sticking from a wooden block. He was obviously used to dealing with people who had no notion of accounts and tax-returns. I had only come in on the off chance of a job. Now he was lining up a whole career for me. Still, he was likable enough and had offered me some work.

'You'll be on the Broadgate job,' he said finally. 'The lads will tell you about it.'

My interview was at an end and I was led away. Later, after I had been briefed about the details, I left the office.

'Film star wages,' I could hear Pete saying loudly as I walked down the stairs.

A few days later I booked myself into a seedy bed-and-breakfast at King's Cross in London and made my way to Liverpool Street Station for my first day as an access worker. We were working on a large metal-clad building above the station. We were subcontractors to a firm who had the overall contract for the cladding of the building. The metal panels covering it had not been bolted into place tightly enough. It was our job to abseil down and tighten each bolt with a preset torque wrench. We quickly calculated this would involve a time-consuming 50,000 bolts.

I soon settled and spent much of my time working with Pat McVey, a friend whom I had shared a house with in Sheffield many years before, just after finishing college. Pat had become an access worker some years earlier, having tired of the life of a penniless climber living on benefits. It was good to be working with someone so experienced, not because the work was particularly demanding, but to make me aware of all the potential pitfalls of such a big building site and to help me avoid getting into trouble. It was soon apparent there was plenty of trouble you could get into.

'This is Loz,' Pat told me on the second day.

I looked across the canteen table at the man who had just sat down. A line of fresh stitches ran along the underside of his left eyebrow. The white of the same eye was bloodshot and both his eyes were blackened. He sat bolt upright, chest out, and leaned over the table to shake my hand very formally, before he broke into a smile. I felt nervous because I knew how Loz had got the injury to his eye just a few days earlier.

Loz always worked with his friend. They had been mates since school-days and were inseparable. Then, over a period of a couple of weeks a series of accidents occurred. While working high on the building, his friend started dropping tools. There was nothing unusual about this in itself, except Loz noticed that this only seemed to happen when he was working below. Their relationship began to sour, words were exchanged and when he dropped a wrench on Loz, he was told he would be in for a beating if it happened again. A few days later a whole kit-bag landed on Loz's foot from ten storeys up, breaking his big toe. Immediately after the incident the pair had marched off together on to a nearby piece of waste ground and set about each other. The fight had been brutal. One had tried to gouge out the other's eye, and he only prevented it by pulling back his thumb until it broke. The pair then retired to a nearby hospital to get their injuries treated. There was no chance of them working together again, and as foreman it had been Loz who had stayed. It was his first day back since the fight.

I seemed to get on well with most of those around me and stay out of too much trouble. There were a wide variety of people working on the ropes. Most of those employed with me were northern-based climbers and cavers, while the existing team were mostly Dagenham-based tradesmen. The two groups of workers contrasted: the tradesmen had learned to abseil for the contract, so while they did their specific jobs well, they were not as confident or fast on the ropes as the climbers and cavers.

The story of how I had cut the rope linking myself to my climbing partner Joe Simpson was doing the rounds on the site. While those in outdoor circles were familiar with the story and the circumstances surrounding it, others were not. I became known as 'Slasher', and the name was scrawled on to my helmet with a marker pen. Men would nudge each other or whisper as I walked past or climbed into the lift with them. A cutting from the *Sun* newspaper with the words 'Mack the Knife' on it, was positioned on the front of my helmet one break-time. But by far the funniest piece of graffiti greeted me one morning as I walked into the canteen. Because of the fear of accidents, posters had been put on the walls. They depicted ropes and anchors with a blunt message below: 'Any interference, with any of this equipment, however minor, could result in this.' At the bottom was a picture of an abseiler lying face-down in a pool of blood. Someone had been round the posters and written 'Slasher was 'ere' over all of them.

At times the continual mockery became wearing, but mostly it worked in my favour. Although the London-based lads were behind much of it, some held me in awe and thought I was some sort of hard man who was not to be messed with. Whenever the ridicule was annoying me, I waited until the workers were over the side on their ropes and then leaned over the parapet above them with a knife in my hands. The look of fear on their faces more than compensated for the discomfort they had been causing me.

The time passed quickly even though much of the work was monotonously repetitive. Many hours were spent sitting on the roof waiting to be told what to do. Not that it mattered. The early summer weather was glorious and it gave me a chance to get to know a little about some of the people I worked with.

Various stories circulated the site about some of the workers and I never knew how truthful they all were. One, I was told, had been a safe-blower as a young man.

'I used to be full of hate and anger,' he told me one day as we lay on the gravel covered roof soaking in the sun. 'But now I am on the Buddhist path to enlightenment.'

If I had known him better I might have laughed, or told him not to talk such rubbish, but he sounded very sincere. I nodded my agreement and kept silent, awaiting his next words of wisdom.

'When I was your age and didn't have any money,' he said thoughtfully, 'I'd fuckin' well nick it.'

Killer strutted the roof-top in a waxed cotton jacket and put beads of mastic between the metal panels fitted along the parapet. He never really talked to me and seemed full of pent-up aggression. I soon learned that putting in thick, smooth and continuous beads of mastic was a very skilled job and Killer was rightly proud of his work. One morning, without thinking I abseiled over the parapet and then swung around on the ropes lower down to get into a working position. I thought little about it until I caught the lift up and arrived on the roof again.

'Killer's after you,' someone said casually.

Then I saw him across the roof-top. He screamed abuse at me and as I walked closer I could see why. My swinging had moved the rope, which had slid right off the edge of the panel and wrecked the bead of mastic he had spent most of the morning putting into place.

'I'm going to fuckin' kill you,' he screamed and if two of his work mates had not been holding him back, he might have tried. I apologised, but it did little to calm him. In the end I moved to another part of the roof and avoided him for the rest of the job.

Each day began in the canteen in a huge Portacabin at the entrance of the site. Then we moved to a makeshift lift fitted to the outside of the building for the ride to the roof. An Irishman with a completely unintelligible accent ran the lift and once the basket was full, slammed the metal gates shut so hard that it made my ears ring.

During breaks people rushed down the ropes to get to the canteen. But the external steel work made it difficult to descend quickly. Loz got bored, and on several occasions when he was working near the top I watched him undo his climbing harness, climb free on to a horizontal girder and then layback up a vertical one to get on to the roof to take the lift down. Once he was out of his harness there was nothing to prevent him falling to the ground.

One day a man working in a cradle on the side of the building grabbed one of our ropes, and in his rush to take his break slid five storeys down to the ground hanging on with both hands. I could hardly believe what I was seeing and he could hardly believe the resulting rope burns, which were right down to the bones in his hands.

On another day I was working near a painter, who kept staring at me and looked amazed when I swung from one window panel to the next.

'Blimey mate,' he said eventually, 'I wouldn't do your job for all the money in the world.'

I could only laugh. I was hanging on two nine millimetre ropes with breaking strains in excess of two tonnes each and the painter was sitting astride a steel girder, eight storeys up and not tied on to anything.

In the evenings we returned to the bed-and-breakfast before amusing ourselves in the local pubs and clubs at King's Cross. But it was not the nicest of areas.

'I've got a lot more calls to make,' I said politely to a man waiting outside a telephone box I was using one night. 'Do you want to use this phone quickly?'

'Cheers mate,' the man said sliding inside the box, before filling the windows with prostitutes' cards and leaving.

We tried to spend more evenings elsewhere in London, but by far the biggest night out was on Thursdays when our two bosses visited. Each carried at least a thousand pounds in cash with them and most of the money was passed over various bars during the course of the evening. I never lasted a full night.

Going on to the roof I often passed men building block walls, which the following day I saw being demolished by electricians or heating engineers to get at some pipes or cables that lay behind. Then the wall would be rebuilt again. Some days we tightened up panels cladding the building, only to loosen them the next day, or fill joints with mastic only to remove it. A constant stream of lorries were needed to take away the skips full of discarded building materials.

Entire days were filled with strange and bizarre events. On one occasion I sat watching a man through a window from outside, who was carefully marking out and then spray-painting yellow crosses on to the huge, bare, concrete floor. Later, when I looked in again, the man was staring at me. Our eyes caught and for a brief moment I could tell he was as puzzled as I was. We both realised we were simultaneously thinking 'what the hell is he doing?' and burst out laughing at each other. To me it just seemed to sum up how ridiculous the whole job was.

'This is crazy,' I told Loz on the roof-top one morning, 'We're being paid all this money for just dicking about.'

'I know, bloody great, isn't it?' Loz replied.

Perhaps it was that this sort of work was new to me, or that having spent so long in Asia previously, but the waste on the site soon began to incense me. It was impossible to square this with the poverty and deprivation I had seen. I knew that the skips of discarded building materials that were routinely leaving the site could build infinitely better shelters than the cardboard and polythene structures in which I had seen so many people living. I pointed out this fact to whoever would listen, but nobody was particularly interested. To most of those involved it was just another job and all that really mattered was getting paid. It took me a while to realise I was taking it all a little too personally. There was little I could do to transfer the wealth, which I saw routinely being thrown away, to a place where I knew it was more needed and appreciated. In London property prices were rising so quickly that the owners simply wanted the building finished, and whenever people work quickly they make mistakes. Here those mistakes translated into skips full of rubbish, and the site we were working on was hardly unique. The London skyline was filled with tower cranes marking similar projects.

What I found most striking while working at Broadgate was different people's attitudes to risk and danger. I could see that the climbers and cavers I was working alongside made very good and safe roped access workers. Their respective sports had given them the rope skills to protect themselves with the utmost safety. But their skills went well beyond the required rope work. Of even greater use was their ability to assess danger and rationalise fear. This meant they were not worried by the heights and exposed positions and were able to calmly deal with problems when things went wrong. In short, they were able to operate effectively in situations that most people would have found very stressful.

Many of the London workers had been on courses to learn rope techniques, but it was obvious they were not completely comfortable with them. Some literally quaked as they went over the parapet, and for a joke we would often pull their ropes tight from the ground, which prevented them from abseiling down any further. Although they had been trained, they could not figure out how to climb back up the ropes either, and they would be left stranded until we loosened the ropes.

Other workers on the site were either unaware of the danger of working at heights or actively courted danger. As a climber I could understand their wish to do this, but did not personally feel the need to because I could get those thrills climbing in more appealing settings. Watching painters wandering around on girders and scaffolders swinging around inside insecure lattices of tubing, I could see that they were quite happy to take risks at work because their lives outside lacked them. They were taking completely unnecessary risks but this seemed a natural thing to do. It was instinctive in certain people and this level of desire had to be fulfilled.

What had made climbers and cavers so good in such settings, however, was their ability to put aside their risk-taking tendencies in a work environment. The record of the roped access business shows this. Even as time goes on, and the numbers of people going into the industry who are not climbers or cavers increases, to this day no roped access workers have been killed in Britain. This compares exceptionally well with other building workers such as scaffolders, steel erectors and steeplejacks who all do similar work at heights, but suffer regular deaths from accidents.

After a little more than four weeks the job came to an end. They no longer required as many workers, and, as last to arrive, I was one of the first to leave. I was not worried. The month's work had served its purpose. I had earned enough money to go away again.

'You want to get yourself an accountant,' one of the lads told me, echoing the words of the boss at the initial interview. 'Claim back some of the tax you've been paying.'

The thought filled me with dread. Ever since I had left for Pakistan nearly three years earlier I had steered clear of the tax and social security people. Now it seemed that far from me owing them, they might owe me money. People kept telling me to sort it out. I obtained some forms from the tax office, which only made me feel even more anxious. I felt sure that the tax people would be so puzzled by me and my lifestyle that they would haul me into the office and question me for several days. The more I thought about it, the more worried I became. Eventually, I saw an accountant who calmly went through my meagre records and sorted them out within about ten minutes. They were probably the simplest set of accounts for three years that he had ever produced. A tax-return was sent to the tax office and after a couple of months I got my rebate. No questions were asked, no inspectors called and no investigations took place. I had worked myself up over nothing.

To me this was a revelation. I had been brought up to have a respect, bordering on fear, of the state. I had lived with the notion that you had to live within quite narrowly defined social boundaries. Now suddenly I knew that the state does not care how you live your life or make your money, so long as it is within the law. Over the years I have come into conflict with a variety of authorities, without really having done anything wrong. I have simply done things slightly differently from others and have not followed what I considered petty or inflexible rules. I could now see a whole host of possibilities and ways of living and marvelled at the freedom we are allowed. I started to think about how many people are limited in thoughts and actions simply through the desire to fit in. The visit to an accountant had been a life-changing experience and reinforced my resolve to live as I wanted to. I felt proud to have joined the ranks of the self-employed, whose work I came to realise is as varied as the people themselves.

At the end of May I left for Pakistan. Like many of Doug Scott's trips, the expedition to Latok I was loosely organised, and once it became clear that the unclimbed North Ridge was plastered in snow and dangerously out of condition, Doug and Sandy Allan decided to leave and go and explore some mountains above the village of Hushe. Rick Allen chose to walk out with them, leaving just me and the Austrian Robert Schauer to climb together.

In a wonderful month of exploring, climbing and filming we attempted to climb a rock spire at the head of the Choktoi Glacier, stood on the top of one of the Karakoram's most remote passes – the Sim La – and finally travelled to the Hushe valley to make the second ascent of a rock spire called 'The Dog's Knob'.

I met up with Sean in Delhi who brought the news that some sponsorship had been obtained and therefore a proposed trip to Pakistan to attempt the first winter ascent of Nanga Parbat would go ahead. We were due to meet the rest of the team towards the end of November, leaving just enough time for a holiday in the south of India after the Shivling expedition before travelling to Pakistan.

I had barely got to the base camp of Shivling before I was struck down with my second attack of hepatitis. Although I was not careful about food and water, I travelled with others with a similar lack of caution, who had not had the illnesses I had, and so could only console myself that I was unlucky. After lounging around at the base camp waiting for some of my strength to recover, I travelled back to Delhi on my own.

'I think you should return to your own country,' my friend the manager of the Blue Hotel told me.

I did not want to return home, I simply wanted to climb. I reckoned I could regain my strength in India ready for the Nanga Parbat trip. I saw a doctor who arranged some blood tests.

'According to these,' he said looking at the sheet of results, 'you should not be standing.'

'Well, what should I do besides avoiding alcohol to get better?'

'No greasy or spicy food,' he said earnestly.

'Are you joking?' I asked, imagining a very limited diet in India. The solemn expression on the doctor's face told me he was not.

I wandered on my own for over two weeks round the romantic fortress towns and cities of Rajastan before returning to Delhi to meet the others coming out of the mountains. Then we all travelled down to Hampi to rock-climb on its wonderful granite boulders, before Sean and I undertook a massive train journey to reach Rawalpindi in Pakistan.

Nanga Parbat is unusual for a large mountain, in that it stands in its own distinct massif, well to the south of the Central Karakoram where all Pakistan's other high mountains are located. From a distance it appears as if the peak hovers above the surrounding red dusty foothills. For this reason it came to the attention of European mountaineers before the other 8,000-metre peaks in Pakistan, which were much more remote. It is one of those rare mountains that people seem compelled to climb. Perhaps it is its sheer bulk: although there are eight other mountains in the world that are higher, none involve more climbing. Nanga Parbat has both the biggest height gain from base camp to summit of any mountain, and the biggest face – the Rupal. Because it stands separate from the main Karakoram Range, surrounded by arid hills, it is also susceptible to terrible thunderstorms. Like the Eiger, Nanga Parbat has over the years become steeped in myth and tragedy. It was first climbed by the legendary Austrian climber Herman Buhl. Tragedy struck him immediately after the ascent, when he stepped through a cornice and fell to his death climbing Chogolisa, further to the north. It was to be the first of a string of accidents and controversies that have dogged the mountain.

The Nanga Parbat team of Polish and British climbers were already comfortable in a hotel by the time we reached Rawalpindi.

'You pair have been in Asia too long,' Jon Tinker said as we walked into the foyer wearing dusty Shalwar Kameezes and distant stares.

The fifty days we spent trying to make the first winter ascent of Nanga Parbat via its enormous Rupal Face were among some of the most gruelling I could remember, and I was confined to the base camp for much of the expedition. After our initial spell of rapid progress on the mountain, the winter began in earnest, trapping us in camp and sending the thermometer plummeting. We huddled around a paraffin stove in a large mess tent, as night-time temperatures dropped to −30 Centigrade. It was even colder at the higher camps. People wore down suits all day long, and for weeks never saw their bodies underneath them. The toilet pit overflowed and the ground became too hard to dig. A huge pile of frozen faeces and toilet paper formed, looking like some sort of modern sculpture.

One morning a massive powder snow avalanche flattened the camp and from then on everyone's nerves were shattered.

For me the final indignity came in the form of a tiny thorn in the sole of my foot. The thorn had entered my foot in the south of India and the wound had never healed properly. The wound went septic and did not respond to antibiotics, forcing the doctor to perform a minor operation to remove the infected flesh. The resulting hole then had to be painfully cleaned and packed with dressing twice a day. When the time came to leave I could still not walk and was forced to ride a mule to the roadhead.

Back in Gilgit, the authorities were worried about our safety. The Gulf War had started, the town was tense and there was much anti-western sentiment. We had to stay in rooms at the back of our hotel to lessen the chance of an attack.

In Rawalpindi a trekking agent friend, Mohammed Ali Chengazi, looked horrified when I hobbled into his office.

'If you have your health, Simon,' he said, 'you have everything.' Once again my body had let me down. In hindsight it would have been more sensible to follow the advice of the hotel manager in Delhi and to have returned home. There I would have been able to recuperate, something I discovered is impossible to do on a winter Himalayan mountaineering expedition. But now I felt like high mountains were my home, and as such I was reluctant to leave them.

Later, Sean and I were surrounded in Chegazi's jeep by an angry mob of demonstrators burning effigies of George Bush and shouting pro-Iraqi slogans. We calmly explained to the ring-leaders that we were Swedish, which seemed to defuse the situation. Everywhere we went there was tension. It was the first time I had experienced many people being openly resentful and hostile towards me in Pakistan, a place I had come to associate with warmth and hospitality. In the end, it was a relief to board a plane and fly back to England.

In terms of climbing, nine disappointing months had passed. I had been to some wonderful places and had some minor successes, but mountain conditions and ill health had prevented any serious attempts on my main objectives. I remembered my friend Dick Renshaw, who had been a member of my first expedition to Pakistan in 1986, saying, 'I think summits are important.' At the time I did not agree with him as I was getting so much out of the whole experience, but as the failures piled up I began to understand exactly what he meant. In a way I had been greedy. I had tried to do too much, without the necessary breaks to recover between trips. My lack of success had left me deeply frustrated, but even though my body was still weakened, all I wanted to do was return to the mountains.

I did not settle at home and wasted a lot of time pursuing various speculative mountaineering schemes and objectives before I received a phone call from Doug Scott.

'How do you fancy coming to the Tien Shan, kid?'

'Where's that?'

'The Soviet bit of Central Asia. Some great peaks and it's only just opened up to western climbers. I've been wanting to go for years.'

'Sounds great,' I replied eagerly. 'I'd love to go.' Then I raced off to search for an atlas to find out where Doug was talking about.

Chapter Eight

Behind the Curtain

I walked slowly, head down, staring at the holes in the snow illuminated by the pool of light from my head torch. Despite the big steps, the slope was very uneven and it required concentration to avoid tripping over. Occasionally, I cast the beam of the head torch further. The slope was covered with varying sized blocks of snow and ice, draped in a blanket of fresh snow. For over an hour we had been walking through the avalanche debris lying in the bottom of a broad valley, and there was no sign of it ending. Sean and I were taking our first outing on Khan Tengri – the mountain we had come to the Tien Shan to climb.

'I don't know about you,' I said pausing for a rest, 'but this place gives me the creeps.'

'I know what you mean,' Sean replied. 'I hope we can get above this crap before the sun comes up.'

'We'll be in trouble if we don't.'

Word had spread about how avalanche-prone the valley that we were now walking through really was and the mass of debris we had seen only reinforced that view. Only a few days earlier Sean and I had talked to a battered-looking Russian climber at the base of the mountain one afternoon.

'I do not understand,' he told us. 'Three times now I have been avalanched in this place.'

'Have you ever considered climbing in the night,' I felt like telling him.

Facing south-east, the valley caught the sun early, and the light and heat stayed on the higher slopes until late into the day. It was these slopes where the majority of the avalanches originated, and the recent snowfall would have loaded them even more.

Eventually dawn came, and the temperature dipped as if to mock the coming sunlight. Our progress slowed as we repeatedly stopped to warm our hands and size up the situation. The debris we had been walking across had fallen from the slopes on Khan Tengri, but the light revealed that the smaller Pik Chapaev also threatened the valley. The first of the sun's rays lit up its summit ridge, exposing a line of horribly unstable cornices which obviously collapsed regularly and scoured the face below. Ultimately, the face ran down into the valley we stood in.

'Have you seen the Russians?' Sean asked.

'Not for hours. I guess we just keep following these steps until we catch up with them.'

'Yeah, but when is that going to be?'

Sean did have a point. The Russian National Mountaineering Squad, who were hosting our visit, were supremely fit. Having already spent two weeks in the mountains they were also acclimatised. We were neither, and were both already breathing heavily.

The sun rose quickly, filling the valley with startling white light. I had barely packed my head torch away, before I was taking out my sunglasses. It was becoming very hot.

As we climbed out of the bottom of the valley we reached a tent, but there was no sign of the Russians. I slumped on to my rucksack, feeling dizzy. My heart was pounding, the veins on my forehead protruding and a headache was forming.

'Do you feel all right?' I asked Sean.

'I'm noticing the altitude.'

'Noticing it?' I replied surprised. 'I'm already shagged out.'

'Well, I don't think we've got much further to go,' he said, getting up.

I watched Sean move slowly and deliberately away from the camp, but it was like I was imagining him in a dream. I woke to the sound of crashing ice and, startled, looked around blinking. A small pillar of ice on the edge of a crevasse above the valley had detached. I watched it smash down the slope and then plough across the trail just 200 metres below me. Enough ice had fallen to have killed or seriously injured anyone in its path and yet I could not care less. Sean was already several hundred metres further along the trail. I watched him for a while and then fell asleep again.

When I woke the sun was burning my face. I pulled a water bottle from my rucksack and eagerly gulped down half of the liquid. Then I smeared some sun cream on my face and stood up. I now felt awful. The cream had taken some of the soreness from my skin, but there was a sharp throbbing pain in the front of my head, which surged with each heartbeat.

I set off, aiming to catch up with Sean, who was now far in front. However, I soon stopped, slumped on to my rucksack and fell asleep yet again. When I woke, I forced myself on by counting steps between rests, but the slope above was demoralising. As soon as I cleared one crest there was another in front, and I only caught rare glimpses of Sean.

I staggered on. The morning disappeared in an interminable haze. I just could not figure out where the Russians had got to. They had told us the previous day that we were going to a camp at 5,300 metres. Although I did not have an altimeter, I felt convinced we had already passed that height. I began to wonder if my mind was playing tricks on me. Had I somehow passed a fork in the trail and missed the camp, or had the Russians forgotten we were following and gone way up the mountain?

'Simon. It's here!'

I looked around wondering if I was now beginning to hear

things. Then I looked up. Sean had appeared on the top of the next rise. With what seemed like the last of my energy I hobbled up and over the crest.

The Russians had already erected the big tunnel tent that they all shared. Someone handed me a cup of tea.

'Do you know what height this is?' Sean asked incredulously.

'Well I think it's above 5,300 metres.'

'It's 5,700 metres,' he said, a worried expression on his face.

'No wonder I feel so shite,' I replied, aware once again of the pounding pain in my head.

I was scared. Just four days before we had been in the foothills of the mountains, not far above sea level, and when we arrived at the base camp at 4,400 metres I had developed a headache. I knew it was pushy to go up to 5,300 metres so quickly, but coming up higher was outright dangerous. In order to feel better, we needed to descend, but it was now too late to go down through the avalanche-prone valley. We were trapped for the rest of the day.

Somehow we put up the tent, crawled inside and lay listless on top of our sleeping bags. I dreamt, hallucinated and in brief periods of lucidity held my aching head. Sean was in a similar state.

'I'm going to give up mountaineering,' he announced at one point.

The day seemed to stretch on for ever. Later in the afternoon Sean left the tent and came back some time later.

'You'll never guess what the Russians are up to,' Sean said, handing me a brew.

'What?' I groaned.

'They're lying around playing chess, reading huge novels, sharing a pan of boiled potatoes.'

I could hardly believe what I was hearing. We had struggled to get this far, carrying only the barest necessities, and we were suffering from that. Our hosts, in contrast, had brought things up the mountain that were far too heavy for me to have even considered.

'How are you feeling now, Sean?' I asked, surprised he had be able to get up and walk around.

'Awful,' he replied solemnly, 'but I don't think I'm going to die.'

I laughed and my head hurt.

In the evening I managed to make it to the Russian tent. Their doctor Yuri gave me some aspirins, which allowed some fitful sleep.

We started down early the next day and by the time the sun was up, we were back on the glacier at the bottom of the mountain. After stashing some spare gear by a group of tents, we carried on down further.

Walking back down the glacier, we passed others going up. The equipment of the local climbers shocked us. They wore corduroy trousers, jeans and check shirts. Some had smock-like nylon anoraks. Most had huge old-fashioned leather boots fitted with homemade crampons that looked like they had somehow been stamped out of tin. Not all of the climbers carried ice-axes, but those that did had ones with lengthy wooden shafts that I had only seen before in old books and on the walls of Chamonix bars. When we first passed people wearing cotton sacks pulled over their heads with pairs of eye-holes burnt into them, I struggled not to laugh.

'They look like the Klu Klux Klan,' Sean said.

'Or condemned convicts,' I replied.

Some of the climbers had sunglasses over the sacks, so we decided they were for protection against sunburn rather than snow blindness. I could only conclude that they did not have any sun cream.

Following the flat, hard ice back to the base camp, I began thinking back over the previous days. I worked out that Sean and I had arrived in Moscow only seven days before.

We had spent nearly three days reaching Moscow by train from London in order to save some money on the price of an air ticket. The ticket inspector had not liked the quantity of our luggage and spent most of the journey shouting at us in Russian. When the train finally arrived at Moscow, we had sat self-consciously for hours on a pile of baggage, waiting for our hosts to collect us, wondering what we would do if they did not turn up.

Then there had been the tours of the city laid on by our hosts, with speeches at every tomb, monument and church.

On Lenin Hill, a popular vantage point for the city, a platoon of Red Army soldiers arrived and started marching around with a dozen women models, while a TV crew filmed them. It was such a strange sight that both Sean and I started taking pictures. Before long one of the camera crew spotted us and walked over to where we were standing.

'Professional model,' he said, pointing at the girls. 'You must pay for photo.'

'No way,' Sean replied.

The man called over another one of the crew, who repeated the demand for money. The pair were big and getting angry. Their demands became louder and more menacing.

'Let's leg it,' I murmured, after a few moments' thought. We took some discreet steps backwards, then turned and ran.

'What's the problem with photos?' Sean asked, as we careered down a flight of steps into a nearby park.

'Who knows?' I replied. 'But they're sure catching on quickly about selling things.'

Everything seemed strange and unfamiliar. At meal times we always seemed to be eating in restaurants where the only other customers were black-marketeers and prostitutes. The plane from Moscow to Alma Ata was delayed, and in order not to lose our seats we had slept on the floor of the filthiest and most depressing airport either of us had ever seen. The language was baffling and as if to make things even more difficult for foreigners, very few businesses advertised their presence in any noticeable way.

In the end, the over-loaded helicopter trying to outrun a gathering thunderstorm to reach the base camp had seemed funny, but I had been relieved when the pilot turned back from the enormous black cloud and decided to try again the following morning. But even with the delays, we had reached the camp at the foot of the mountain very quickly. On previous Himalayan expeditions the walk-in had always taken several days.

Soon we were down the glacier and back into the sprawling International Camp. More people had arrived in the time we had been away. A street of tents now stretched away from the main mess tent.

Our own smaller camp was separate, and I was happy to avoid the cosmopolitan gatherings in the big tent. With over a dozen members, the Russian team was large by my own standards. In addition to the climbers there were two cooks. The team members' tents were spread out around our own smaller mess tent. We walked across to the large frame tent that the Russians had set up for our use and unzipped the door.

'I think we might have brought too much of that stuff,' Sean said pointing at the huge pile of food blocking the porch.

'You might be right. Still Alexei's enjoying it.'

We both laughed. We had brought the extra food all the way from Britain, because we had heard there were food shortages. We expected that sweets and chocolates, which we used a lot in the mountains, would be in particularly short supply. In the main camp the food was quite basic, but as state-sponsored athletes, our hosts received privileged treatment and good food. We had not needed to eat as much of our own food as expected and had been giving our spare chocolate to one of our cooks, Alexei, who normally worked in a beer hall in Moscow. Several times a day he would take bars as gifts to girls in nearby camps, and Sean and I would speculate about what favours he managed to get in exchange for them.

I threw my rucksack into the mess, amazed at what a tip the tent had become in just a few days.

'Right, I'm off for a sauna,' I said hoping that the tent would be miraculously cleaned up by the time I got back.

I grabbed a towel and set off back to the International Camp. Down below the mess tent was a wooden hut with a boiler on the side. I wondered how it had been transported, and reckoned they must have flown up prefabricated pieces in helicopters. Inside there were hot showers and a small wooden sauna room. I sat inside, letting the aches of the previous days' exertions sweat out of me. It was strange sitting on the wooden bench, naked and hot, looking out across a glacier, surrounded by huge mountains. However, I did not feel the need to remind myself of what was outside, as some did, by rushing out of the door and diving into a nearby glacial pool.

When I returned to the tent, Sean was sitting among the gear and food with his feet in a bowl. I recognised the smell of mustard coming from the hot water in it.

'There's some cough sweets somewhere in this lot, you know?' I said, pointing at the food boxes.

'You're okay. I think this is working and I'm going for a sinus massage later.'

'Suit yourself,' I replied trying to hold back my laughter.

Sean had been suffering with a cold ever since we had arrived at the base camp and had gone along with a course of herbal remedies offered to him by the Russians. I had tried some of their medicine for myself and had eaten a ball of a black tar-like substance that I was told would help with acclimatisation. It had tasted vile, and if my suffering in the tent the previous day was anything to go on, it had not worked.

Later, as the sun set, we sat outside watching Khan Tengri in the fading light. The mountain's symmetry looked superb at any time of the day and I remembered that when Sean and I stepped off the helicopter, we had shouted, 'we'll have to climb that,' in unison. In the late afternoon, the light went off the eastern side of the mountain, outlining the arrow-straight profile of the south ridge that faced the camp. The ridge we had chosen to climb was known as the Marble Rib, after the rock that formed the top section of the peak. Later in the day, the rock of the south west face glowed a warm orange. I could not recall having ever seen a more beautiful mountain. Despite all the disappointments and setbacks of the previous year, I felt positive. I imagined myself standing on Khan Tengri's perfect summit.

'Shall we go back up tomorrow?' I asked, without averting my gaze.

'You bet,' came the unhesitating reply.

In the mess tent that night we discussed our plans with Rick. Rick Allen and his wife Alison had joined us in Moscow, having taken the easier option of flying from Britain. Doug Scott, who had organised the whole trip, had been forced to stay behind to meet the deadline for a book he was writing. Rick and Alison had come on Doug's Latok trip the year before. I had enjoyed climbing with Rick, whose quiet-spoken manner disguised a steely climbing drive. Rick intended to climb to the top with the Russians, but was keen to climb some of the way with Alison in order to acclimatise further first. They decided to follow us up.

We did not leave until the late afternoon, as the day had been particularly hot. Higher up, the previous days of sun had turned the thinnest snow lying on the ice into a zone of mush which formed a front right across the glacier. There was no way round it. For several hundred metres we waded through ankle-, knee- and thigh-deep slush running with water. Despite wearing waterproofs and gaiters we were soaked up to our waists. It was not a promising start.

When we reached the camp, we set up our tent and got on with the business of making drinks and food. Rick and Alison arrived just as it was getting dark. Alison had struggled in the slush, and water on the outside of their clothing was already starting to freeze. It was obvious they were not going to have a comfortable night.

That evening there was thunder and lightning, followed by wind and snow.

'We're going to go down,' Rick shouted into the entrance of our tent in the morning.

'We're going to sit it out,' I shouted back.

The wind and snowfall were intense all day and we had to get out of the tent a couple of times to clear snow away. But despite the weather, we planned to go up the following morning.

We were woken by the alarm at 2.30am, but it was still snowing heavily.

'Ah, let's go back to sleep,' Sean said.

When we woke at 9.30 it was eerily quiet and still.

'I think it must have stopped,' I said enthusiastically, unzipping the tent door before undoing the porch. As I did so, snow avalanched into the entrance.

'What were you saying?' Sean said smugly.

'Shit. It's up to the top of the porch.'

We stared out above the piled up snow at the desolate scene. Not far away some Russians were digging their partially collapsed yurt-like tent out of the snow. Visibility was no more than ten metres and it was still snowing hard. The weather in the Tien Shan was proving very fickle and I was amazed that there could have been so much snow in such a short space of time.

'I guess we'll have to go down when this lot clears,' I said wearily.

Sean nodded his agreement and lit the stove,

'Well at least we don't have to go far for this,' he said, scooping up a pan full of snow.

By late morning the storm had died down and the cloud started to lift. We dug our way out and packed away our damp belongings and the wet tent. Then we set off. The thigh-deep powder snow would have been wonderful to ski on, but was very hard work to walk through. It was impossible to see exactly where we were going, so we simply walked in what we felt was the right direction. When the cloud finally lifted, we laughed at our tracks which zig-zagged down the glacier.

What had been a three-hour walk on the way up took over six on the way down. When, exhausted, we finally ploughed our way back into camp the sky cleared completely, revealing a huge plume of snow blowing from the summit of Khan Tengri.

I woke the next day to the sound of laughter. Light was streaming in through the tent's plastic windows. I dressed and stepped outside. The brightness hurt my eyes and I hurriedly put on my sunglasses and viewed the scene more comfortably. The sun was now blazing from a clear, dark blue sky. There was not a breath of wind, even on the summits. Everywhere was white, with hardly a rock showing. The place looked pristine and new. I had never seen a more beautiful panorama.

The camp was buzzing with activity. People's spirits had lifted with the storm and now everyone was out enjoying the perfect day. Sean and I were the last to rise. I waved at some of the Russian climbers across a small valley from our tent, who sat in swimming trunks, soaking up the sun's rays outside their tents. They waved back, smiling. New tracks crisscrossed the camp through the fresh, sparkling snow.

I stared up at Khan Tengri until the two beautiful Siberian girls, who worked as cooks in the International Camp, walked past in bikinis. With their long, straw-coloured hair and opaque white skin they looked strangely out of place in such surroundings. They walked over a small moraine ridge and lay down on foam mats in a little hollow.

Later, when the sun's rays seemed to have an unnatural power, I was surprised to see the Siberian girls still sunbathing. Others had spent an hour or so outside and then wisely returned to their tents. I was not surprised to see them an hour afterwards, walking back towards camp, with their skin a fiery red colour. When I next saw them several days later their faces were covered in scabs and their lips ringed with cold sores. They had spent the intervening time in their beds, delirious with fever and pain, from the worst sunburn I have ever seen.

Later in the day I noticed that everyone around seemed to be packing their rucksacks. I strolled across to Rick's tent and found him sorting through his gear.

'What's happening?' I asked.

'The Russians are going early tomorrow morning. I'm going to go with them.'

I felt a slight pang of envy. The weather looked set fair for a few days, but because we had stayed up at the higher camp Sean and I needed another day's rest. We also needed to allow time for the avalanche-prone slopes at the foot of the Marble Rib to clear of snow.

'What will you do?' Sergei asked me at dinner that night.

'We'll go up after another rest day.'

He nodded as in agreement, but looked like he was thinking hard. As leader of the Russian National Mountaineering Squad, Sergei Efimov seemed a very thoughtful man, whose slight frame obviously disguised a great deal of physical strength.

'I will get some climbers to go with you,' he said.

'No thanks, we'll climb on our own.'

'Just two?' he looked puzzled.

'Yes, we have a small tent for just two people. For us this is normal.'

'That is very interesting,' Sergei said, looking like my comments had been some sort of revelation. 'It is not normal here.'

I could understand that as the leader Sergei Efimov felt responsible for our safety and relied on the benefits of climbing as a large team, but to us that would take some of the challenge and enjoyment out of it. We wanted to climb as a self-contained team of two, completely responsible for ourselves.

'But you will take a walkie-talkie?' Sergei asked matter of factly.

'No, we won't need one of those either.'

Sergei looked at me like I had lost my senses.

The following day, after all the Russians had gone up, Sean and I came to the mess tent to watch the team coach Valeri making radio calls to the climbers on the mountain. We asked the translator to tell us what he was saying. He was giving orders to those on the mountain. Personally, I had not been attracted to mountaineering as a communal activity. For me, it was about freedom of both thoughts and actions. Decisions always had to be made after consultation with the partner or partners who you were climbing with, but it was never really a matter of one telling the others what to do, and the idea of following instructions from a man who was not even on the mountain seemed dangerous. I wondered if the differences in our climbing styles mirrored some of the differences in our societies.

Late the following day we left the camp. I felt strong and motivated. We set the alarm for 2 a.m., but when we woke it was snowing lightly.

'Come on, let's give it a go,' I said to a reluctant Sean. 'If we wait for the weather here all the time, we'll never get anything done.'

Not long after we set off, the sky cleared and we walked swiftly up what we had come to know as 'Death Valley', this time without any of the problems of our first visit. It was good to reach the 5,700 metre camp feeling normal. We set up the tent and relaxed in the sun.

In the late afternoon the Russians and Rick arrived. They had reached the summit earlier in the day. We congratulated Rick on becoming the first British man to climb the mountain.

'We're going to go on Pobeda in three days' time,' Rick explained. 'Once the mountain is climbed, we'll all have to go.'

'So if we're going to get a chance at climbing Pobeda, we'll have to do this quickly?' I asked.

Rick nodded. I thought that our own schedule was flexible, but I was beginning to realise that here things were done in a group or they were not done at all.

'What should we do?' Sean asked.

'I'm for bagging the mountain and getting a chance at Pobeda. Besides I'm not too happy about traversing that slope to get to the bottom of the Marble Rib.'

Sean looked across at the slope lit up in the afternoon sun, littered with avalanche debris, and thought for a moment before saying, 'Let's do it.'

I wanted to climb the Marble Rib because it was the most compelling way to get to the summit. But now reaching the summit had become more important than the route we took, or the style in which we climbed. This way we would also get a chance at Pobeda.

In the morning Rick and the Russians went down and we moved up slowly towards the col at the bottom of the West Ridge. Once we were on the ridge itself we followed it to a notch at 6,400 metres, which Rick told us provided the best camp.

The camp was very exposed. Sitting right on the crest of the ridge the tent caught the full force of the wind. There was never any real danger of us being blown from the ledge, but it was necessary to brace ourselves when the biggest gusts pushed in the walls of the tent. The continual sound of the flapping fabric got inside my head and as a result I slept only fitfully through the night.

It was a relief when the early morning light began filtering through the tent fabric. I lit the stove and made some drinks.

'Come on, Sean,' I said prodding his sleeping bag, before passing him a mug of juice. 'It's time to get going.'

'I suppose we'd better,' he groaned.

Neither of us were very good in the mornings, but the wind would allow us no rest in the tent anyway. We dressed inside, and then I put my harness, boots and crampons on and stepped out into the day. The sun was now up, but provided little heat. The biting wind was bitterly cold. The Russians who had been following us for the previous days were now negotiating their way through some steep, small rock buttresses up above. Looking at their primitive tent flapping wildly in the wind, I imagined their night had been worse than ours. I guessed they had moved early to get warm.

I struggled to free some gear clipped to a piton, as Sean climbed out of the tent. The gates of the karabiners had frozen in the night and it was difficult to open them with my mittened hands. Finally, the gear separated and I was able to remove some ice-screws.

'Give us a hand with this,' I shouted, pointing at the ice surrounding the tent.

We knelt down and placed some of the screws in the ice, before anchoring the tent to them. Then we removed our ice-axes from the guy-lines that had previously been holding the tent in place.

'That should do it,' Sean said, throwing some spare food into the tent from his rucksack. The tent was going to act as a store for the day and neither of us wanted to return and find it had been blown away.

I set off. Snow-covered shelves were separated by steep, compact walls of marble. Some sections were fixed with pieces of decaying rope and others were not. It was hard to know which was more dangerous, to climb relying on the rope or to climb without it. To start with I stopped frequently to remove my mitts and blow into my hands, but I soon got warm and built up a rhythm. We made good progress.

Sometimes I paused and looked down to see where Sean was and to admire the view. At first the day was clear, but cloud soon boiled up from the valleys below. To me the cloud only seemed to make the place more atmospheric as occasionally it parted to reveal a dramatically sunlit peak behind.

At the top of the ridge, a long easy-angled traverse led away towards a series of steps that led to a steep wall below a basin. At the bottom of the wall I stopped, worried by what lay above. The condition of the rope was shocking. I could choose between three on the steepest section and they were all rotten. The sheaths of the ropes had obviously gone a long time ago and only a few strands of core remained. I considered waiting for Sean to belay me with the rope I was carrying, but it was very cold and my desire to reach the summit was driving me on. Instead I simply clipped my jumar to the thickest rope, and a karabiner to all three, in the hope that if the rope supporting my weight failed and I fell, the remaining two ropes might just hold me. It seemed a slim chance. Blanking out my fears I jumared quickly, but I was still relieved when the angle eased and the rotting rope came to an end. With a sigh of relief I clipped myself into a piece of rope I could trust.

The basin was filled with very deep snow. Hauling up through it was hard work and I was grateful for the team of Russians in front, who had broken a trail.

As I pulled out of the basin and on to a ridge, the full force of the wind hit me once more. Every step became a struggle. A snow arête led to a short rock wall and the rope I had been following ended. Above were easy-angled snow slopes, but it was impossible to tell how far they stretched into the swirling cloud. I staggered on, having to crouch occasionally during the most ferocious gusts of wind. I hardly noticed the Russians passing me on their way down. Then the snow ended and I found myself walking on fine snow-blasted gravel that was somehow frozen into place. It was awkward ground to move over and I kept catching my crampons, but the angle was easing. This time I felt sure I was going to make it. Soon I would stand on the summit of Khan Tengri. Teetering on, I slumped over my ice-axe each time I needed to rest.

Then suddenly, over to my right I noticed a tripod sticking out of the snow. A few flags fluttered from the metal. I moved towards it and as I got closer I could see the ground beginning to drop away on all sides. Drawing level with the tripod, I realised it was over. A feeling of both relief and joy flooded through me, as I thought about all the illnesses, setbacks and disappointments that seemed to have blighted my climbing in the previous few years. Now it had all been worth it. I was on the summit of Khan Tengri.

The clouds were speeding over the top, but through occasional breaks I could see other peaks. The huge bulk of Pobeda to the south stood clear for much of the time.

Then I looked round for Sean. He was hunched over his axe, meandering up the slope just below. I waved at him and he veered towards me. Soon he stood beside me and firmly grasped my hand as we cowered backs to the wind. We took turns to take some photographs and I hoped Sean did not get close enough to notice my freezing tears. Then, without a word we walked away from each other and spent a solitary minute or two savouring the summit and the fleeting glimpses of the land below. My tears were really flowing now and occasionally I had to rub my eyes to free my eyelashes, which had frozen together.

As I walked around, I remembered the moment earlier in the day, when before the cloud had rolled in, I had looked into the distance. As I looked at the horizon filled with peaks, rolling gently away to the foothills in the north, I had felt I could see the curvature of the earth. It had seemed a profound moment. I had realised simultaneously both how lucky I was to be up here looking down at such beauty, but also how small and insignificant I was. It was a liberating feeling.

Back at the base camp, Rick told us they were going to attempt Pobeda the following day. Their schedule could not be changed. Having let us climb on our own on Khan Tengri, Sergei was adamant that we should climb with the Russian team on Pik Pobeda. The problem with the normal route on the mountain was the three-kilometre ridge above 7,000 metres, which had to be traversed to reach the summit. When parties hit bad weather or got sick from altitude while on the ridge, they had to make the long traverse back, before they could descend to safety. Many people had failed to do this and Pobeda had gained a reputation as a killer. We were told seventy bodies lay buried in the snow along the ridge.

After a wholly inadequate night at the base camp, we repacked our sacks and wearily followed our Russian hosts up a separate fork of the Inylchek Glacier towards the huge menacing bulk of Pobeda at the head of the valley.

Chapter Nine

Homeward Bound

I was surprised to see the Russians returning to the camp so early. I had only completed my own slow, painful descent a few hours earlier, after the frustration and disappointment of my accident high on Pik Pobeda. I still felt angry about the Russians hanging on the rope below me, which had probably been the cause of my fall, but as I saw the men coming into camp I vowed to say nothing. There seemed little point in criticising their actions. They had only been doing what they considered normal and safe.

I had not been expecting them to return until the following day and reasoned that in the time available they could not have possibly reached the top. Sean and Rick would be following and I felt disappointed for them. They had missed their chance to go to the summit of Pobeda. Still, now I would get my ankle looked at sooner, by the doctor who had also been with them on the mountain.

Using my ski-poles as crutches, I hobbled across to Yuri's tent. He saw me coming and opened the door flap to let me in. I sat down on a small chair and removed the sock from my injured foot. I winced with pain as Yuri twisted my damaged foot one way, then the other.

'Why did you come down?' I asked.

'There was too much wind for the summit today.'

Although the weather had been good at the base camp and the sky clear, I knew that to follow the exposed ridge to the summit required a day of light winds. Now as I looked closely at the mountain I could see plumes of snow blowing from the ridge.

'I think it is only soft tissue damage,' Yuri said, finishing his examination.

'What's that then?'

'Some strained ligaments. Possibly some are torn.'

It was reassuring to hear from a doctor that my injury was not as bad as I had first feared. For the two days it had taken to struggle down Pik Pobeda after my accident high on the mountain, I had been convinced some bones were broken. Looking at the swelling and bruising on my ankle and foot, it was still hard to believe that none had been.

Yuri filled a plastic bag with snow and put it around my ankle.

'Last night your friend had a problem.'

'Which friend?'

'Sean.'

'What was the matter?'

I felt a growing anxiety. The Russians had a habit of continually understating things. We had laughed about it before, but now I was worried. I suddenly understood why Sean and Rick had not arrived back with the others.

'He had pulmonary oedema, but is all right now.'

Yuri had done nothing to diminish my fears. Pulmonary oedema is a potentially fatal condition which can be caused by gaining altitude too quickly. As a result the lungs fill with fluid and slowly suffocate the victim. There are drugs that can be administered to slow down the effects of the oedema, and drinking plenty of liquid also buys more time, but the only effective long-term treatment is to go down. Generally, a descent of 1,000 metres will be more than sufficient. Once a lower altitude is reached, the lungs reabsorb the excess fluid and a recovery is made.

When Sean finally walked into the camp he looked tired and drawn. Rick had stayed to keep him company.

'How was it?' I asked as he staggered into the tent and threw his rucksack on the floor.

'Oh, man,' he sighed, 'I thought I was going to die last night. My lungs were gurgling each time I breathed in and out. Rick was a star. He stayed awake and made me brews, and by drinking enough I managed to reverse the effects.'

'Sounds like you were lucky.'

'Yeah, but I wasn't the only one to have a bad night. There were five Russians huddled in a tent next to us, dossing down under three sleeping bags. It was really windy and cold. Even they wanted to come down this morning.'

'Well at least you're all down safely.'

'Sure, but I'd really have liked a chance at climbing that mountain, and the Russians say we're leaving the day after tomorrow. Something about training schedules, the team, that sort of thing.'

'Yeah, I know what you mean.'

It had all been too quick. We had been rushed into the mountains, by those who were already acclimatised, to follow an inflexible schedule. Sean was angry because he had not been fully prepared. That lack of preparation had cost him the summit and nearly his life. It could have been avoided if he had been allowed to act on his own ideas and intuition, rather than follow an inflexible schedule. Probably all he needed was an extra day or two resting in base camp.

When the Russians had hung on the rope beneath me and caused my accident, I had been very angry, but now I was calm. After my disappointments of the previous year, at least I had reached a summit. I just had to accept that these were different people with values very different to my own. Sometimes what they were doing seemed dangerous or crazy and at other times it had been a revelation, a learning experience. I knew we were lucky to visit such a place and be with such people after the years of isolation their state had imposed on them. Personally, I can only see the benefits that travel and contact between different people bring. To me, the exchange of ideas allowed both sets of participants to grow, develop and learn from the experience, and if not, then at least to understand each other better. And on another level, the contacts made offer possibilities for commerce and trade. Yet these were not the reasons why the Soviet Union's leaders prevented most of their people from travelling abroad, or coming into contact with foreigners. They did so to prevent them from seeing the truth. The free movement of people in and out of the country would have allowed an exchange of information their leaders wished to hide.

We spent the following day lazing around the camp and that night a celebratory meal was prepared. It was a fantastic evening. The food and vodka flowed and our hosts took it in turn to sing ballads while playing the guitar.

At the end of the meal Sergei stood up and made a formal speech thanking everybody for taking part. Rick replied for our team and another reply followed. The game of speech ping-pong went on for some time as each was painstakingly translated. I washed down biscuits covered in caviar with glass after glass of neat vodka.

'What will you do next?' I asked Sergei, when the speeches finally finished.

'This autumn we will go to Cho Oyu and next spring to a new route on Dhaulagiri.'

'Well it's good you can travel,' I said, knowing there were now no restrictions.

I knew that in future it was going to be very difficult for them to find the money to go to Nepal, but I felt confident they would get it from somewhere. I knew from my own experiences that mountaineering could be as addictive as a hard drug, and that like drug users I would beg, steal or borrow to fuel that addiction. I remembered years before meeting a group of Polish mountaineers in Gilgit in the north of Pakistan. Unlike the Russians, the Poles had no restrictions on their travel and as a result they became a dominant force in Himalayan mountaineering throughout the

1970s and '80s. However, they always struggled with money as their own currency was worthless abroad. They developed all sorts of elaborate trading to get the local currency they required. The climbers I met in Gilgit had brought 5,000 pairs of Polish training shoes to sell to provide the necessary funds for their expedition's food and porters. It took them two weeks of hard bargaining to sell the shoes, which remained in the Gilgit shops for several years afterwards. I sensed the Russian climbers also had a similar focus and passion, which would be useful to them as their circumstances and country changed. At least they had something to strive for even if it was only climbing a mountain. Alternatively they might follow the path of some of the Polish mountaineers I knew who, once communism collapsed, had taken up opportunities denied them before and become successful businessmen.

The vodka flowed late into the night and I left while I was still able to do so. Later, I was woken by Sean shouting abuse at the full moon.

In the morning we were told that a helicopter would come and collect us that afternoon. Our time in the mountains had come to an end. We spent the morning packing.

Yuri was interested in buying my jacket. Many of the climbers we had seen had woefully inadequate clothing by our own standards and although those in the National Mountaineering Squad did have some modern western gear, they were still looking for more.

'I'd like forty pounds,' I told him. I could see him converting it into roubles in his mind. His face dropped and he shook his head. He could not afford anything like that amount of money. 'Have you got anything to swap?' I continued, trying to do my best to help him out.

Yuri emptied out a kit-bag on to the ground. I picked up a strange pair of ice-axes. They were just handles with a hook-like blade. With no wrist loops or shafts they would be incredibly strenuous to use. Yuri took them out of my hands and demonstrated their use. He thrust them backwards and forwards above his head very quickly.

'For speed climbing,' he explained.

I knew that here they had ice climbing competitions, where a top rope was put down and competitors climbed as quickly as possible, while someone took in the rope. Whoever climbed the route the fastest was the winner. The coaches used the results to help them select their mountaineering teams. The idea of competing for a place on a mountaineering expedition seemed a little frightening to me. I preferred simply to go along with some friends. Here mountaineering was very much like any other sport and the authorities had found ways of quantifying and measuring performance. People were added or dropped from mountaineering squads on this basis.

I looked again at the axes and handed them back. They were of no use to me.

'Have you got any ice-screws?' I asked. Yuri went to his tent and returned with a bag of shiny new titanium ice screws. I picked one up. They were wonderfully light. At home they were prohibitively expensive, if you could obtain them at all. 'How about ten for the jacket, okay?' I offered, expecting to be bartered down.

Yuri shrugged his shoulders. I got the impression he did not care how many I took and had no idea of their monetary value, but I did not have the heart to ask for more. I felt I had a very good deal.

Sean had watched the whole transaction. Within minutes he had swapped his own jacket for twenty screws. Then in a frenzy of trading around the camp he exchanged most of his spare clothing, driving very hard bargains. He quickly amassed nearly two hundred ice-screws.

I laughed when Sean showed me his haul. I knew exactly what he would be thinking. With the profit from selling the ice-screws, he could pay for another expedition.

'I reckon I'll get ten pounds apiece for these screws back home,' he said.

Back in Moscow we returned to the flat in the suburbs that we had stayed in when we arrived. Rick and Alison went on the tour of the city, but Sean and had seen enough and found it much more interesting simply to watch people in the street.

Communism was faltering and you could sense the place was on the verge of great change. Small private businesses were starting. There were kiosks selling imported chocolate and cigarettes, as well as private restaurants and bars. People stood on street corners and openly changed money, even though officially it was illegal outside state banks. In squares and parks, groups gathered and talked politics. And while most people simply carried on as if nothing was happening, there was a feeling of energy and excitement.

We were taken to Arbat Street to see a market that had recently been set up. People were selling Russian dolls and paintings, while men nearby played accordions and violins to accompany the dancing of tiny Georgian girls. The owner of one stall had painted 'let's trade' on to a blank canvas. Nobody seemed to be buying much, but compared to many of the city's other grey, drab streets and empty supermarkets at least this place was lively and colourful.

To me, it seemed strange that a system that guaranteed people food, health care, education, work and houses, in short welfare from the cradle to the grave, could suddenly find itself so unpopular. Surely, this was exactly the sort of security people often said they would like, or strived to reach? But as we walked around the Moscow streets I did not see happiness in people's faces. I saw weariness, tiredness and boredom.

A McDonald's Restaurant had recently opened in the centre of the city and was very popular. We went along to look at the queue outside, and I wondered why a government would prevent an individual or company from opening a shop to sell burgers. Sean, a committed vegetarian, was not impressed.

'It's sad,' he said, looking at the line of people stretching several hundred metres down the road from the restaurant.

Earlier we had watched drivers removing their car windscreen wipers as they parked. There was a shortage of replacements and people had taken to stealing them. Some foods were in short supply also, but it seemed it was possible to get any number of burgers if you were prepared to queue. No doubt the novelty would wear off, but for now McDonald's were one of the few companies providing people with what they wanted.

Suddenly the difference between physical needs and desires seemed very sharp. People's needs are fairly simple, but what they desire is much more complex. Here people longed for the consumer goods that westerners take for granted, and for an end to state control and interference in their lives. Yet I knew many at home who longed for more state interference, particularly against big business, which they felt increasingly powerless against and saw as only adding to the insecurity in their own lives. Then there were others like myself and the mountaineers that I had met while in the Soviet Union who were seeking something different, something not tangible or material, something that was simply a feeling. Perhaps it is in our nature to want what we cannot have, or is difficult to obtain. I could see that there were many sorts of people in each society and those different people with their different desires, drove society in a particular direction at any given point in time.

Here it seemed people were weary of a system where their basic physical needs were met, but they could not strive for anything more. But it went further, not only were some of these basic needs provided for by the state, they were also controlled by it. However, the state had done little to facilitate people's desires, aspirations and dreams. The government had put arbitrary limits on what achievements people could make, what risks they could take and what excitements they could have. It was hardly surprising the system was on the verge of collapse. What was more surprising was that it had lasted so long.

The queue provided Sean with some good photographic material and he wandered up and down taking pictures. Most did not seem to mind and some even smiled for the camera. Then he found an old lady at the back of the line with a bag and started taking a lot of pictures of her. The lady seemed agitated.

'I don't think she appreciates your art,' I said, as the woman picked up her bag and started advancing towards us. She thrust her hand out, demanding money. Sean shook his head. The lady moved closer, dipped her hand inside the bag and pulled out a knife.

'She's a nutter,' Sean said, as the old lady came at us with the knife. Luckily, she was not very fast and we simply walked quickly to keep away from her.

'How embarrassing,' I muttered, as the lady continued the chase. People were now pointing at us and laughing. We had to walk the entire length of the queue before the knife-wielding old lady ran out of energy and we were able to get away.

There were two days before Rick and Alison's flight home and we decided to make the most of them by getting out of Moscow and visiting Leningrad. The city was a big improvement on Moscow and we all enjoyed the wonderful architecture and a visit to the Hermitage – the Winter Palace of the Russian Tsars.

We stayed with a young couple who both worked in the university. They explained how until very recently it would have been illegal for them to have foreign guests staying in their flat. They were nervous about what the future held for them, but also excited and optimistic about new opportunities. They dearly wanted to travel abroad and it had not been possible under the old system.

'Any news about our train tickets?' I asked Sergei as he met us off the train at the station in Moscow.

'Maybe we get you ticket to Warsaw or Berlin.'

Sergei had been trying to get us tickets home ever since we had arrived in Moscow. The only way the tickets would be cheap was if a Russian bought them and paid for them in roubles. At first he had said there was no problem, then that it was impossible and now we were getting another version of events. We sensed he was struggling, but did not want to let us down.

'Listen Sergei,' I said. 'We can get ourselves home once we are in western Europe. Anywhere will do.'

'I will do my best, but I cannot promise anything,' he replied solemnly.

'We'll give it one more day and if you can't come up with anything we will have to open our wallets and buy flights home,' Sean said.

Rick and Alison had returned home that day and we were beginning to get bored with waiting in Moscow.

When Sergei visited the following day, he said he needed to make a telephone call to check on our tickets. I was not holding out much hope and began wondering if buying air tickets a few days earlier would have saved us time. Then he rushed into the room.

'Quick, we must go. Your train leaves in one hour.'

'Where to?' I asked.

'London, I think.'

We hurriedly packed and caught a taxi into town. At the station we met a man who produced two tickets from a battered brief case. He did not look very trustworthy.

'How much for the tickets?' Sean asked.

'Five hundred roubles each,' said Sergei.

I could hardly believe our luck and quickly paid the man in case he had made a mistake. Sergei hurried us to a platform, helped us on to the train and found us an unoccupied sleeper compartment. Once all our kit-bags of equipment were inside, there was precious little room to sit down. We barely had time to say goodbye and thank Sergei before the train pulled out of the station.

We dragged the bags around on the floor for a while to get them comfortable and then lay on top of them. I pulled the tickets from my pocket.

'Do you think these are going to work?' I handed them to Sean, who inspected them.

'They look like old-fashioned toilet paper,' he said shrugging. 'We'll just have to see, I guess.

We did not have to wait long before the inspector came

along. To our surprise he simply pulled a page out of each ticket booklet and went away again. The pieces of paper got us as far as the Polish border. Then to our further amazement a further page got us to Warsaw.

Over two days the tickets took us through Berlin, across Germany and into the Netherlands. We boarded a ferry at The Hook of Holland, got on another train in Dover and finally arrived in London. As the train pulled into Waterloo Station, Sean and I stood up, slapped the out-turned palms of our hands together and burst into fits of laughter. Having changed money at fifty roubles to the pound our tickets to travel from Moscow to London had cost us £10 each.

We had not really done anything illegal, apart from changing money on the black market, and the government had already given up trying to control that. I felt particularly proud. With our collective cunning accumulated after years of living at the margins of society while somehow paying for our mountain addiction, we had somehow hoodwinked both the communist and capitalist systems simultaneously.

I was not so happy paying a further £19 to travel back from London to Sheffield.

Epilogue

It is many years since the events in this book took place. Since then communism has collapsed and the Soviet Union has ceased to exist. Kazakhstan is now an independent sovereign state. Global telecommunications, travel, trade and the internet are revolutionising all aspects of our lives.

While writing these words I have enjoyed rediscovering old friends, climbing partners, people from many different cultures, and remembering some of the wonderful places that I have been fortunate enough to visit. However, it is the mountains that have provided my most intense experiences. With very little effort, I can recall precise moments, indelibly etched into my mind. I only have to close my eyes and I can crawl on to the summit of Ben Nevis after a hard day's climbing and watch again the sun setting behind snow-capped peaks over the Western Isles, while a full moon rises to the east in a matching blaze of colour. Alternatively, I can transport myself to a Karakoram campsite and sit and gaze at the meteors flashing across a star-filled sky, or I can simply toast a summit in a Chamonix bar.

Many mountaineers struggle to come to terms with why they climb. I have never had such dilemmas. I know I climb because I love to have adventures. What puzzles me more is why I carry on sometimes in the face of unbelievable adversity.

On occasions I have tried caving, paragliding, skiing, canoeing and mountain biking and enjoyed them all, but for me they do not provide the level of excitement and adventure that I find in mountaineering.

But what is adventure? The dictionary I have in front of me gives three definitions as a dangerous enterprise, a novel or exciting experience and a commercial or financial speculation. For me, travelling to an unknown place to ascend an unclimbed mountain provides the challenge, risk and uncertainty that I consider are the necessary ingredients of a true adventure, but I accept that most people would not have to go to such extreme lengths to satisfy their own desires. However, the feelings of pleasure and excitement I get from anticipating an adventure and planning it in my mind, are almost as intense as the experience itself. These are my dreams.

Perhaps for most of us, then, adventures are games where we try to live out some of our dreams. And though true adventurers probably follow these dreams and desires to the exclusion of much else, they give a positive focus and direction to their lives. But we all dream and plan our own adventures.

Many of us plan the same long-term adventure; to find a partner, to make a home and to raise children. We can almost take this for granted, as if it is a certainty. Those that aspire to things outside of this norm are often considered eccentric, strange or weird, while those who want to pursue the peaks of mountains, the bottoms of oceans or the depths of caves, and are willing to risk their lives to do so, are sometimes considered totally mad. Yet whether we court risks or not, nothing is certain.

I feel some people recognise that by putting an element of danger, uncertainty and challenge into their lives, they regain a feeling of freedom that they might not have even realised they have lost. Freed from the hold imposed on us by the state, employers, community and family, people involved in an adventure can feel empowered and actually in control of their own lives. But there is also a strong current against this line of thinking. There is also a culture of not taking responsibility for ourselves and blaming others for our own mistakes.

Our wealth can provide us with comfortable living conditions and advanced health care, which prolong our lives. However, this does not guarantee that we will all live in perfect health and until the average age of death. Many people in our society do not see things this way and behave as if living healthily to an old age is a right, rather than good fortune. When they or their families are adversely affected by what I would consider the normal risks of being alive, of being human, they seek scapegoats through the legal system. To me, it seems they wish to blame someone and to be financially compensated for a loss of contentment and happiness that is impossible to measure in monetary terms. I see many of these people as simply after revenge. In bygone times I could imagine such matters being settled by fights and killings. Now people use the courts.

The collapse of communism proved to me that you cannot cherry-pick culture. If people are stopped from doing too many of the things they wish to, by fear, legislation or peer pressure, then society as a whole will stagnate and ultimately collapse. Societies progress, grow and develop through innovation – new thoughts and actions – and in my opinion the greater variety of people you have, the more likely this is to occur.

There are only small numbers of adventurers like myself. To some we are inspirational figures who show that anything can be achieved, and to others we are dangerous lunatics who should be banned from practising our pastime. I sometimes wonder what useful purpose people like myself serve, but in the end I realise that I am just a part and product of the society that I live in. I simply pursue my dreams and desires in a way different to most others.

I have no doubt that it was an adventurer that led some of our ancestors out of the Rift Valley in Africa, and successive generations of them that encouraged migrations across the world. Others set sail across oceans or walked over ice to reach some of the most remote and hostile places on our planet. I do not believe that people's only motivation for these movements was simply to look for food, to gain status or to seek their fortunes. For me personally, this has never been the case. I feel certain that I would both be wealthier and regarded more highly by the majority of others if I had simply stayed at home and taken up a professional career. And I am sure that most adventurers over the ages have not benefited materially or financially from their actions. I think they simply relished the challenge and the chance to discover what lay over the horizon.

Throughout history exploration and migrations have changed, depending on the wealth of societies and the technology of the day. Those left behind have probably always simultaneously ridiculed and envied those that have moved on. In Europe, people scoffed when Portuguese and Spanish mariners went to cross the Atlantic. Some said they would sail off the edge of the world. In fact they discovered the New World. Others went east, and while European colonial history is not something to be proud of, the trade that resulted from this exploration still plays a vital part in our lives today. Doubtless, some thought Charles Darwin was mad to sail off in the *Beagle*, yet his two years of travels and adventures resulted in his theory of evolution. In more recent times we have the Wright Brothers flying their aeroplane and astronauts blasting into space.

We have evolved over millions of years to live with uncertainty and danger and to adapt to changing conditions and circumstances. I believe that over time humans have developed the desire to explore, discover, and experience things new. This allows us to stay one step ahead of changing conditions and dangers, to shape our own circumstances and to limit some of the uncertainty in our lives. It is this ability as adventurers that has made humans so successful and it is this ability that continues to drive the change and innovation that is now central to us all.

This success has also brought problems. Our greatest challenges for the future are improving the living conditions of the world's poor, while stemming the unsustainable damage we are doing to our environment. It will take the co-operation and exchange of ideas of the widest possible groups of people to be able to achieve this.

I am writing these last words just days before flying to South America to board a yacht in the town of Ushuaia on the southern coast of Tierra del Fuego. Together with a group of friends I plan to sail west along the Beagle Channel, to reach an isolated fiord that will give access to some of the most remote mountains in the world. This to me is an adventure. And while I do not pursue adventures in such a blind and obsessive way as I did when I was younger, I cannot imagine life without them. They define who I am and how I grow, develop and learn as a person. I know that without these adventures my own life would be boring and frustrating.

We live in amazing times, where communal wealth and global communications make it easier for us to do remarkable things. The possibilities and opportunities are almost limitless. They are a wonderful gift, and in order to embrace that gift, all we have to do is open our minds.

Acknowledgements

Over the years I have shared my adventures with many friends, associates and workmates and I would like to thank them for contributing so much to my life and for providing the vivid memories I have drawn upon to write this book. I would also like to thank the numerous kind and generous people who have helped me wherever I have travelled. I have been lucky to have met and spent time with such a variety of interesting and inspiring people. I am eternally indebted to my parents for the constant help and support thay have given to a rather difficult and unconventional son.

I have received much assistance for my mountaineering expeditions from various companies and organisations that form the commercial and administrative core of the climbing community. In particular I would like to thank DMM Ltd, Rab Down Equipment, Wild Country, The North Face, Karrimor, Buffalo, Troll and Berghaus who provided the specialist equipment and clothing essential to such ventures. The British Mountaineering Council and The Mount Everest Foundation gave much needed financial assistance to some of the expeditions mentioned in this book, for which I am very grateful.

My own selection of photographs have been much enhanced by inclusions from Pat McVey, Steve Razzetti, Sean Smith and

Mike Searle. Thank you for taking the trouble to use your cameras when I was not using my own, and for allowing me to reproduce the pictures here.

I do not find writing easy and require the support and help of others to produce a readable finished product. Special thanks go to Jane for putting up with my regular writer's tantrums and for still loving me, and to Tony Whittome at Cape for all his work as my editor. I would also like to thank Ruth Halsey, Val Randall, and Jackie Williams for reading the manuscript and their suggestions for improving it.

Finally, I would like to acknowledge the inspirational and pivotal roles that Mark Miller and Tony Colwell played in my life. It was predominantly Mark who opened my eyes to the opportunities for adventure that lay within the world's more distant and remote mountains, and it was Tony – my first editor at Cape – who encouraged me to write. Mark died on a Pakistan International Airlines plane that crashed into a hillside near Kathmandu in September 1993. Tony died of cancer in October 2000. This book is dedicated to their memory.